Divorce

Frances Sieber

TEACH YOURSELF BOOKS

For UK order queries [...] Bookpoint [...]on Park, Abingdon, Oxon OX14 4TD. Telephon[...] [...] re open from 9.00–6.00, Monday t[...] with a 24 hour message answering service. Email address: orders [...]t.co.uk

For USA & Canada order queries: please contact NTC/Contemporary Publishing, 4255 West Touhy Avenue, Lincolnwood, Illinois 60646–1975, USA. Telephone: (847) 679 5500, Fax: (847) 679 2494.

Long renowned as the authoritative source for self-guided learning – with more than 40 million copies sold worldwide – the *Teach Yourself* series includes over 200 titles in the fields of languages, crafts, hobbies, business and education.

A catalogue record for this title is available from The British Library.

Library of Congress Catalog Card Number: On file

First published in UK 2000 by Hodder Headline Plc, 338 Euston Road, London, NW1 3BH.

First published in US 2000 by NTC/Contemporary Publishing, 4255 West Touhy Avenue, Lincolnwood (Chicago), Illinois 60646–1975 USA.

The 'Teach Yourself' name and logo are registered trade marks of Hodder & Stoughton Ltd.

Copyright © 2000 Frances Sieber

Typeset by Transet Limited, Coventry, England.
Printed in Great Britain for Hodder & Stoughton Educational, a division of Hodder Headline Plc, 338 Euston Road, London NW1 3BH by Cox & Wyman Ltd, Reading, Berkshire.

Impression number   10 9 8 7 6 5 4 3 2 1
Year   2005 2004 2003 2002 2001 2000

CONTENTS

INTRODUCTION

In 1975, *The Times* published a letter I had written asking that 'The Master of the Rolls (Lord Denning) does not change the law before the law exams take place the following week'. The same sentiment applies now with the number of future changes which are being proposed.

This book is aimed to be an explanation of the law as at February 2000 and includes references to expected changes in the law and procedure (see Chapter 6). The intention is to explain the jargon and the legal process. It is not, and cannot be, an explanation of every situation which can arise on marriage breakdown and divorce, although it tries to deal with the more common ones. The examples given are situations accepted by many courts, but courts do have different practices and some courts may make changes to the procedures described here.

It may seem obvious, but a divorce can only take place between people who have gone through a legal form of marriage. It does not include co-habitees or couples who have undertaken a purely religious marriage. This book applies to divorces in England and Wales only.

The book cannot replace independent legal advice. If a solicitor is consulted, it is important for the solicitor to be a specialist in this area of law, and for both the client and the solicitor to be able to work together. At some point, unpalatable advice may be given and the client must have the confidence to accept it. The clients must always remember that it is their divorce; their long-term relationship with the former husband or wife, and possibly children, is at stake. It is for them to instruct the solicitor on how the matter is to be dealt with.

The use of husband and wife are used arbitrarily in the book and the terms can be interchanged as is the presumption over which party is the petitioner or respondent. 'He' and 'she' are also used interchangeably.

The book is divided into six chapters. Chapter 1 covers the preliminary stages leading up to divorce, Chapter 2 covers the process of divorce and Chapter 3 deals with finance. Because this latter aspect is usually the most important and because it is the most complex, this part is proportionately longer than the other parts. It is the financial aspect of a divorce that usually generates the most conflict and that incurs the bulk of the legal costs. Chapter 4 deals with the arrangements for the children in so far as they relate to a divorce, and Chapter 5 with costs and legal aid. Chapter 6 seeks to set out the forthcoming changes in the law but it must be born in mind that this is ever changing.

The writer's approach, having been a family lawyer for twenty years, is to reduce conflict on divorce rather than increase it and the advice given is written with this in mind.

1 | PRELIMINARY STAGES

In this section, the initial stages of a marriage break-down are considered, including what steps can be taken to try to save the marriage; what outside help is available; and what effect could the break-up of the family have on the individual members and children. It includes practical advice such as finding a solicitor and taking initial steps to protect property and money.

Is the marriage over?

Preliminary considerations

Before embarking on a divorce, it is necessary to consider whether the marriage is over and cannot be saved. The full effect and consequence of a divorce should be considered. Do the parties really want to throw out the marriage or – with more effort – could it be saved, or its difficulties overcome? Could an acceptable lifestyle be allowed to develop within the marriage? Is there a problem with communication between the parties, which could be solved with outside help?

Divorce is not easy. It is a major upheaval and one of the most stressful events anyone can go through. It usually involves a house move for one or both parties. Remember, the time is not always right, for all sorts of reasons. These should be considered carefully before embarking on a divorce. It may be better to live in an unhappy marriage for a little time, so that when there is a divorce, the outcome (emotionally as well as financially) is better.

Consideration should be given to the following.

■ Is the situation so bad within the marriage that the marriage should be ended?

■ Are there outside factors creating undue pressure on one party which is having an effect on the marriage, such as work commitments, illness, drug or alcohol abuse? Could these be resolved with outside help?

■ Is there a history of violence, and if so, when was the last incident and what caused it? Was one party to blame or were both responsible? Is this a marriage where there has been recurrent violence?

■ Do the parties appreciate the financial effect of a divorce? There are economies of two people living together. Two homes will have to be acquired and maintained from the same income that previously provided for one home. If there are children they will require accommodation with both parents at an additional cost. There can be extra costs incurred for the children's travel between parents.

■ Is this a good time to embark on a divorce? Are there other matters which should be dealt with before adding the difficulty of a divorce?

■ Is there any urgency for a divorce, such as a need to remarry?

■ Could the divorce, i.e. the legal process, be allowed to wait until the parties have adjusted to the situation and tensions have perhaps abated?

■ What will be the effect on the employers of the parties? Most employers view divorce by an employee as bad news, as it will detract from the individual's ability to carry out his work. The divorce takes time, liasing with lawyers or dealing with the matter in person and attending court. Is there a promotion in sight which could be jeopardised? Is there a possibility of redundancy or situation which may make a person's job more vulnerable?

■ Have the children been considered? Are there going to be any changes in the care needed for them, such as the youngest child attending full-time school, or children completing their secondary education? Is the youngest child going to be eleven years old, which has an effect on the court's approach to the carer's ability to work? (see page 56).

■ What will be the effect on the children's education? Are there public or other major exams in the foreseeable future? Is a child approaching puberty, which is considered a bad time for a child to experience divorce.

■ What ages are the parties? Is one or other party going to turn 50 or retire in the near future? This has an effect on pension rights and the ability to draw capital lump sums out of a pension (see page 121).

■ Is it to one person's advantage to have a divorce quickly, or to the detriment of the other?

■ Are the parties' financial positions going to change in the foreseeable future?

■ Does one party have financial difficulties? Is there a possibility of bankruptcy in the next few years? Consider the effect of a bankruptcy or an individual voluntary arrangement (IVA) on the financial settlement (see page 112).

■ Should there be a speedy divorce to try to protect assets from creditors?

■ Is one party likely to inherit money on the death of a relation in the foreseeable future which could effect the outcome of the financial application?

■ Is there going to be a change in the law which will assist, or is any prospective change adverse?

■ Has everything been done by the individuals to try to save the marriage, so that in future years they will not feel guilty about the marriage break-up.

Outside help

Before the marriage is over, and certainly while the intention of the parties is to preserve the marriage, the help of trained counsellors can be constructive.

The parties should consider counselling, either singly or preferably jointly, to see if they can resolve the difficulties between them. Counselling can sometimes identify the problems that one or other party may have which have nothing to do with the marriage, but which have a direct impact upon it. However, if one party wants counselling and the other refuses, there is no way a person can be forced to go to counselling. Counselling can also help a party come to terms with the end of the marriage and to cope with the emotional effect of a marriage break-up. It can act as a very good support to a person going through divorce.

Counselling can be obtained through various organisations such as The Tavistock Institute, Relate, or London Marriage Guidance (see page 181 for addresses). The counsellor needs to have the appropriate specialist training for family matters. Each counsellor will have individual procedures and will advise, usually at the first assessment meeting, how they recommend the counselling should be carried out – whether in weekly sessions, sometimes with two counsellors present, or in some cases, that counselling is not appropriate. A counsellor may see the parties in separate meetings or together.

Trial separation

A trial separation can sometimes help bring about a reconciliation by giving the parties some distance so that they can work on the relationship without feeling pressurised. It can help make one or other party realise what life would be like if the marriage was over. The following points may be useful to bear in mind.

- A separation of this kind should not start as a result of a row or argument with one person walking out.
- It should be discussed by both parties and agreed in advance what the purpose of the separation is, the period it is to last, what contact there is to be between the parties during the period of separation, and arrangements for seeing the children, if any. Sometimes a period of 'courtship' can help.
- The financial arrangements during the period of separation should be agreed upon in advance.
- It may be difficult to arrange if alternative accommodation is not available to one party for the period. Sometimes friends or relations will assist.

- ■ Neither party should be subjected to pressure from outsiders, however well-meaning, during the period.
- ■ It can help if there is counselling during this period.
- ■ If the parties agree to live together again, counselling should be used to try to help overcome future difficulties.
- ■ As it can be disadvantageous to the party leaving the matrimonial home, it must be agreed, preferably in writing, that the trial separation will not affect the occupational rights of the person moving out. It follows that the person remaining in the property must agree not to change the locks on the doors or deny access (unless there is some other legal reason to do so).

Deed of Separation

This is a legal document between the husband and wife in which they record that the marriage is at an end, but that they do not want a divorce immediately. It confirms that they are going to live separately in the future. Very often a Deed of Separation is entered into when the parties want to divorce but do not have the grounds for an immediate divorce (adultery or behaviour) and wish to live separately for a period of two years after which time they can divorce (see page 32). Alternatively, a Deed of Separation can be made when the parties want time to consider whether or not the marriage is at an end, or where there are financial reasons which make it desirable to delay a divorce.

A Specimen Deed With Draft Financial Order Annexed

THIS DEED is made the day of ____ **BETWEEN** ___ of (hereinafter called 'Mr X') of the one part and ___ of (hereinafter called 'Mrs X') of the other part

WHEREAS:

(a) Mr X and Mrs X were married on the ____ and ____ they have decided to live separate and apart as from the ____ 0000.

(b) Mr X and Mrs X have each taken separate and independent legal advice on the matters referred to in this Deed.

NOW THIS DEED WITNESSETH and it is hereby agreed and declared by and between Mr X and Mrs X as follows:

1 Mr X and Mrs X will hereafter continue to live separate and apart.

2 Mr X and Mrs X agree that after a period of living apart for two years Mr X will petition Mrs X for divorce on the basis that the parties have lived apart for the period of two years and Mrs X confirms that she will consent to the divorce, it being further agreed that that there shall be no order for costs on the petition.

3 It is agreed that the children YY and ZZ do reside with Mrs X, and Mr X shall have staying contact every alternative weekend and two weeks in the school summer holiday and one week in each of the Christmas and Easter holidays.

4 It is agreed that the terms set out in the Minute of Order attached hereto are accepted in full and final satisfaction of each party's actual or potential claims of any financial nature whatsoever against the other or the other's estate whether by way of capital or income, or pension provision, including for the avoidance of doubt but not limited to such claims pursuant to section 23 and 24 Matrimonial Causes Act 1973, section 17 of the Married Women's Property Act 1882 (as amended and extended), the Trusts of Land and Appointment of Trustees Act 1996 and the Inheritance (Provision for Family and Dependants) Act 1975, and it is intended that in the context of the divorce proceedings Mr X and Mrs X will invite the court to make an order in the terms agreed.

5 Mr X and Mrs X confirm that they have given full financial disclosure of their respective means and have received independent legal advice on the terms contained herein.

6 Any variation of this Deed shall only be effective if recorded by a Supplemental Deed executed by both parties.

7 The parties shall bear their own costs of and incidental to this Deed.

8 This Deed shall be governed by and construed in accordance with the law of England and Wales. The invalidity or unenforceability of any provision of this Deed will not affect the validity of enforceability of any other provision and any invalid or unenforceable provision will be severable. Further and in any event if any application is or has to be made to the court pursuant to this Deed and the Courts of England and Wales have jurisdiction at that time and the courts of one or more other legal jurisdictions also have jurisdiction to entertain the application, Mr X and Mrs X agree that they intend the Courts of England and Wales to deal exclusively with such application.

SIGNED as a Deed the day and year first before written by by Mr X in the presence of: _____

SIGNED as a Deed the day and year first before written by Mrs X in the presence of: _____

If the parties agree at this point to the terms of a financial settlement, a draft financial order can be annexed to the Deed. The financial application is only finalised, however, when a court makes a final financial order; and the court is not bound to make a final order in the terms of an agreement between the parties. In particular, if there have been changes in the circumstances of one or other party, such as a serious disabling illness, then the court will consider the matter afresh.

If it is to give effect to any financial agreement incorporated into a Deed of Separation the court will need to be satisfied that:

■ the agreement was not entered into under duress;

■ full financial information had been exchanged. Such information includes the capital, income and liabilities of the parties;

■ it has full information on whether the parties have other partners and intend co-habiting or remarrying;

■ both parties have had independent legal advice before the agreement was signed so that they are aware of the legal effect of the agreement.

The Deed can include details of the arrangements for the children, for example, who they are to live with and what contact the other parent is to have with them.

Effect on children

Children suffer both in an unhappy household and in one where there is a divorce. However, there is research which shows that children will achieve better in a home with an unhappy marriage, (though not a violent one), than one where there is a divorce. It is even thought that children achieve better where there is a bereavement of one parent than where there is a divorce, because of the long-term effect of a divorce. The following points need to be considered where children are involved.

- Children may react in all sorts of ways. There could be behavioural problems, resulting from a need to seek attention. They feel insecure and may even feel guilt for the break-up of the marriage, thinking that they are responsible.
- Children can be overprotective of one or other parent and can feel rejection by the parent who is leaving. Children can be sensitive to the emotional upset of one parent and are vulnerable to being used by one or other parent.
- Young children can be extremely clinging and more childish behaviour can occur. Bed-wetting can be a manifestation of their anxiety.
- With older children, there can be violence, withdrawal and a hatred for one or other parent.
- Where one party has committed adultery, the hatred can be directed at that parent and the new partner. If they set up home together, the relationship between the child and the new partner can put intolerable burdens on that relationship.
- Sons can become very protective of their mothers, particularly if the mother is emotionally upset by the divorce.
- Divorce can be particularly hard for a child when that

child is at puberty, as it can lead to the child finding it difficult to form stable relationships in adult life.

■ Where the child is suddenly deprived of seeing one parent for a period, he can suffer a form of bereavement at the loss of contact.

■ It is desirable for the children to see both parents frequently. If this is not possible, a regular pattern of contact should be established as early as possible. If meetings are not possible, contact by telephone, letters and e-mails (if appropriate) should take place.

First steps to divorce

Advising the partner

Once it has been decided that the marriage is at an end, the person who has made the decision should tell the other. It is preferable if both parties accept that the marriage is over so that sensible steps can be taken to the next stage. This frequently does not happen. It is important to try to minimise the distress caused at this time. If the party intends to use a solicitor, it helps if one is found and consulted before the final decision to divorce is communicated to the spouse. It is also desirable that the decision is communicated personally by the person taking it, and it is courteous to advise a partner that a solicitor has been instructed and that he or she will be writing to them. It is appropriate to advise a spouse before a divorce petition is issued that a petition is going to be issued and sent to him or her. It is good practice for a solicitor of one party to write to the other party, or their solicitor if known, before a petition is issued (see specimen letter below).

Example

Dear Sir/Madam

Re: Mr/Mrs _____

We have been instructed by your husband/wife and we understand that as a result of difficulties in your marriage over the last __ months, that he/she has now concluded that the

---

marriage is at an end. We understand that even though there have been attempts to overcome the problems, your husband/wife has concluded, with great regret, that a reconciliation is not possible. We should stress that this decision has not been reached easily by your wife/husband.

It is our client's intention to petition on the basis of your (adultery/behaviour). In the context of the divorce proceedings the arrangements for the children and the financial arrangements need to be dealt with and we trust this can be dealt with in a constructive and amicable way.

We recommend that you should seek independent legal advice and accordingly invite you to pass this letter to your solicitors. We look forward to hearing from you or your solicitor in the near future.

Yours faithfully

Instructing a solicitor

A person is entitled to 'act in person' (represent him or herself in the court proceedings). There is no obligation to instruct a solicitor. Where a person does represent him or herself, the court will be careful to ensure that that person knows what the effect is of any stage in the process and, in particular, does not enter into a financial order without knowing the legal consequences. A person can file his or her own divorce petition and the county courts produce a helpful booklet explaining the procedure and the steps that need to be taken. The necessary forms can be obtained from the court or from a legal stationer, or the internet (see page 182). Having a solicitor should make the procedure simpler, but a specialist family lawyer is recommended who can offer his or her experience with the procedure and can perhaps help defuse some emotional situations.

A specialist family lawyer can be found through the following means.

- The Law Society's Family Law Panel of accredited family lawyers.
- The Solicitors Family Law Association (SFLA) that

was set up in about 1982 by family lawyers to encourage a conciliatory approach to divorce and whose members are specialists. Local lists of members can be obtained from the secretary (see page 181 for address). The SFLA has also launched its own accreditation scheme in 1999. Advertisements appear in the Yellow Pages under the SFLA for local solicitors.

■ Local Citizens Advice Bureaux keep lists of local solicitors who undertake family work and those who undertake legal aid work.

■ There are various directories of lawyers and some will show whether firms undertake family work. Searches can even be done on the internet.

In choosing a solicitor it is important that the client will be able to work with and feel confident with him or her. At some point, unpleasant decisions may be necessary and if there is no confidence it will make the acceptance of advice more difficult. Some people see several solicitors before deciding who to instruct.

■ Make sure that the solicitor seen at the first interview will be the person who will deal with the matter on a daily basis, or that the person who will be acting is introduced at that meeting.

■ Consider how the solicitor will communicate. How readily available is the solicitor when needed? How will the solicitor make contact? There can be difficulties if both parties to the marriage are still in the same house. Could mail be interfered with? Will telephone calls be overheard? Sometimes letters can be sent to a work address, a neighbour or relation's address or by e-mail.

■ Remember that it is the client who gives instructions and the ultimate decision on how a matter proceeds is for him or her to dictate. The lawyer's function is to advise on the different courses available and the likely decision the court will take given the circumstances. If a client wishes to take a hard approach, he or she should make sure that the solicitor will stand up and fight for him or her. If the client wants to take a more

conciliatory line, he or she needs to make sure the
solicitor will take this approach.

■ Make sure the solicitor is not going to be overbearing
and take actions without explaining why and getting
the client's agreement to the proposed course first.

■ Beware – some solicitors will automatically take an
unnecessarily hostile approach which is likely to
increase the tension and animosity between husband
and wife.

Dealing with children

The children should be told of the decision to separate and divorce
by the parents early on, rather than overhearing others discussing it.
If possible, both parents should tell the children together of their
decision and the children should be reassured that the reason for the
separation is that the parents are unhappy living with each other,
and that both parents love the children and remain committed to
them. It is important that the children are protected from the
animosity that can arise in divorce and however bitter one parent
may feel towards the other, neither parent should be critical of the
other in the presence of the children. Sometimes one parent, usually
the mother, may take out her anger on her husband by being
obstructive over contact with the children, for example, not being at
home at a pre-arranged time for the hand-over of the children or
cancelling contact at short notice on a pretence such as that a child
is ill. This does not help the long-term relationship between the
parents nor with the children. It is useful to notify a child's school if
there is a divorce so that the school can act as a support to the child,
away from any parental conflict.

Protecting property rights

If the husband and wife own property in joint names, neither can
sell the property without the consent of the other. The property is
therefore protected already. If there is uncertainty, a search can be
made at HM Land Registry for the title number of the property and
'office copy entries' of the entries at the Land Registry can be
obtained. If both parties' names appear in the Title Absolute section
as joint proprietors, the property is in joint names.

If, in addition, the property is held as 'joint tenants', and this is shown by a statement in the title document that 'either being able on the death of the other to give a valid receipt for monies', then the position is that if either dies the other will automatically inherit the property, 'the right of survivorship'. Where there is a divorce it is usual practice to stop the automatic right of survivorship on the death of either party. This is not always appropriate. There can be disadvantages in severing the joint tenancy, particularly for the party who is dependent on the other.

Example

Second marriage, no children of this marriage. House in joint names. Wife aged 55, husband aged 75, in poor health and with children by former marriage. If a Notice of Severance is served, the wife will not inherit the property by survivorship. It is not in her interest to serve a Notice of Severance.

If it is wished that the interest passes to the estate of the one who dies and passes under a will or under the rules of intestacy, then a Notice of Severance can be served. See specimen below.

Notice Of Severance Of Joint Tenancy

TO: _____

OF: _____

(We, _____ , of _____ , as duly authorised Solicitors of and for and on behalf of our client _____ (or I,) _____ your fellow joint tenant at law and in equity of the property set out in the Schedule below hereby give you notice pursuant to the Law of Property Act 1925 section 36(2) that he/she (I) desire(s) to sever your joint tenancy in equity so that as from the date of this notice you and he/she (I) shall hold the said property on trust for sale, for your selves, as tenants in common in equal shares as if there had been an actual severance.

We (I) request you to acknowledge receipt of this Notice by signing and returning the duplicate notice enclosed herewith.

SCHEDULE

All that property known as ____ registered with HM Land Registry under title no ____

Dated this ____ day of ____ 2000.

The notice must be served on (sent to) the other owner and the Land Registry must be notified.

If a property is held in the sole name of, say, the husband, he could sell the property without the knowledge or consent of the wife. However, a wife can protect her position by registering a notice under the Family Law Act 1996 (formerly under the Matrimonial Homes Act 1983) and lodge the notice on the prescribed form with the Land Registry. If the title number is not known, an index map search can be carried out to obtain the number.

Making a new will

In most marriages each party leaves his or her property in a will to their spouse, or alternatively it will pass under the laws of intestacy. When a marriage breaks down, both parties are likely to want to make new wills leaving their property to other people and in particular to any children. On the decree absolute (the final stage of the divorce, see page 44), any gift to the former spouse or appointment as a trustee will be cancelled automatically. That stage can take some months, even years, to reach.

On the breakup of the marriage, consideration should be given to making a new will which provides for the immediate needs of the spouse but protects the bulk of the assets. There is a statutory provision which gives a spouse or former spouse the right to receive reasonable financial provision on the death of the other out of their estate. Some provision may therefore be appropriate to avoid such a claim and a statement can be included in the will stating that the provision is intended to satisfy any such claim. If a party is a member of a pension scheme, a direction may have been given to the pension trustees requesting that the death-in-service benefit and widow's or dependant's benefit be paid to the spouse. Consideration should be given to changing the instruction, either at this point or in the context of the final financial settlement.

Joint finances

Immediate consideration should be given to all jointly owned assets of the parties. The following may need to be considered in order to protect them.

- If there are joint bank or building society accounts, can the spouse take out all the money? Can he or she overdraw the account? Can he or she be relied on to operate the account sensibly? If there is a joint bank account, both parties are responsible for any overdraft. The accounts can be frozen or made subject to the joint signatures of both parties to protect the monies in the account.

- Where there is a bad record with a bank, some banks will automatically freeze all joint accounts which can cause immediate practical difficulties.

- Set up new individual bank accounts for the husband and wife as soon as possible into which their salaries/maintenance are paid before any joint bank account is frozen.

- Ensure that any funds, whether joint or held solely, are secured until the financial aspect of the divorce is dealt with. It may be that this can be done by agreement between the parties, or if there is a concern that one party may dissipate or hide assets, then an injunction should be considered (see page 111).

- Where there are credit, store or chargecards in one party's name, but on which the spouse has a card, the account will need to be closed to ensure that the account is not incorrectly used. Sometimes the spouse will agree not to use the account and hand over the card. Sometimes the spouse will refuse to co-operate, in which case the card issuing company will need to be advised and requested to close the account.

Religious considerations

In some religions divorce is not recognised, such as the Roman Catholic Church. In others, divorce is not encouraged. Some churches have their own counselling services to try to prevent marriages breaking down.

In the Jewish faith, remarriage between parties where one has committed adultery with the other, before the divorce, is not permitted. To name the co-respondent in such circumstances is considered vindictive.

In some faiths a special religious divorce is required. Some foreign-born Muslims require a Muslim divorce which is registered with their respective embassies to allow remarriage. Jews require a Get, which needs the co-operation of both the husband and wife to obtain, and this is given by the Beth Din. As the court deals only with civil divorce and not religious divorce, if a religious divorce is required, the application for it and co-operation in the making of it, should be included by way of an undertaking in the financial order.

Example

In respect of a Jewish divorce as follows:

And the petitioner and respondent undertake to apply for and take all steps necessary to obtain a Get.

Mediation

While there will need to be a legal divorce, issues of children and finance could be dealt with by mediation rather than by the court.

The aim of mediation is for mutual agreement to be reached after full disclosure of the husband's and wife's respective financial positions. The mediator will help the husband and wife recognise the needs of the other party and find an acceptable solution to the problem. Solicitors can give advice on the alternative courses available and on the legal position in conjunction with the mediator. Usually there are a number of sessions, and at the end an agreement is signed setting out the terms and the financial position of the parties. Any mediated settlement will still require incorporation into a financial order, in order to finalise the matter.

In respect of a child(ren) dispute, the terms can be agreed in writing and no formal court order may be required at all. Child mediation may need to be an ongoing process: the position may change as children adapt to the new situation and their needs change as they get older. As a result of changes to the way legal aid, is granted in divorce, if a person is eligible for legal aid it will not be granted until the person has attended an information meeting which is aimed at directing a person into mediation (see page 169). Legal aid is available to cover mediation on divorce and court-based mediation now forms part of the financial relief procedure in courts operating the Pilot Scheme (see page 74).

Tax implications on divorce

There are special tax concessions for married couples. On divorce, the treatment of tax changes is as follows.

- The married man's allowance which is payable while the parties are legally married ceases. There is limited tax relief of 10% of the additional personal allowance if maintenance continues to be paid to a former spouse after divorce. This benefit will be abolished from 2000/2001 tax year.

- The capital gains relief on transfers between husbands and wives living together is lost, if, for example, shares are transferred from one spouse to the other, during the marriage, while the parties live together capital gains tax does not arise and the recipient takes the shares at the value of acquisition by the transferor. After divorce, in a similar transfer, capital gains tax will be payable by the transferor.

- Inheritance tax is not payable on gifts between spouses. Once there is a divorce, the widow is no longer a widow, and inheritance tax will be payable on any gift to her by the former spouse.

- Capital gains tax does not normally arise on the sale of the matrimonial home. On divorce, provided the non-resident party has not made an election in respect of another property, capital gains tax should not be payable on the sale of the property, provided the former spouse has continued to live in it.

■ Mortgage interest relief will be lost if the non-resident spouse is paying the mortgage, which is being abolished in 2000.

■ The sole parent with whom the children live should receive the child benefit and an additional sole parent allowance is payable.

■ Before 1989, tax relief was available on the full amount of spousal and child maintenance, and payments were usually made net of tax so that the recipient received the payment less the basic rate tax. If the recipient had no other income, he or she claimed a tax rebate and thereby got the benefit of the personal allowance. The relief was also available to each child of the family so that there was a saving of the personal allowances and lower rate tax bands for each child. Since 1989, all payments have been made gross and tax may have had to be paid out of the money received. The tax relief in these old cases is limited to the amount of the relief available in 1989. This benefit ceases at the end of the 1999/2000 tax year.

The loss of the capital gains tax relief can be serious where there are substantial assets to transfer between the parties. It may be possible, where there is a high degree of co-operation to achieve an early settlement and implement it before the divorce (and within the tax year in which the parties separated).

Example

Husband and wife have 50% each in family owned company, now worth £3 million. On divorce the husband is to keep the company, so wife transfers her shares to him. If done before divorce and within year of separation, no tax payable. If done after year of separation or divorce, tax to pay on disposal.

Emergency applications

Where there is the need for urgent applications to the court either to protect money (see page 111) or because of violent or abusive behaviour, the court can give an injunction on an urgent application. Where a spouse has been violent or threatening, it should be possible to obtain a 'non-molestation order', i.e. an order that he does not molest, assault, harm or intimidate the other.

Where there has been a serious incident or the behaviour is such that it is having a seriously adverse effect on the spouse or child(ren), then an 'occupation order' may be granted, which excludes the other spouse from the home.

2 | THE DIVORCE PROCEDURE

The section covers the legal process of divorce, including who can divorce, what the steps are and includes a description of the new divorce law. An announcement is due in 2000 over whether and in what form the new divorce process will be introduced.

Who can divorce?

It is a legal requirement for there to be a divorce in England and Wales that there must have been a valid marriage, recognised by the English courts. That excludes people who are co-habitees or in a same-sex relationship. It also excludes people who have been married in a purely religious festival in this country. Alternative remedies to divorce including nullity, judicial separation and presumption of death are also considered below.

Has there been a legal marriage?

The requirement that the parties are legally married means that they must have gone through a legal ceremony of marriage.

The court recognises marriages entered into in other countries provided the marriage is lawful within that country. It does not recognise purely religious marriages, such as a Muslim marriage, in this country. The court will recognise a polygamous marriage, provided it was a valid marriage in the country where it took place. A polygamous or potentially polygamous marriage cannot be entered into in this country.

Jurisdiction requirements and considerations

The court can divorce people who are either domiciled in England and Wales and/or where one or both have been habitually resident in England and Wales for 12 months immediately preceding the presentation of the divorce petition to the court.

The concept of domicile is that a person can decide which legal system he or she wishes to be bound by and the court has to determine where a person is domiciled. This can be a country that a person visits intermittently rather than lives in all the time. This happens, for example, where people have homes in more than one country. One test used to determine domicile is to ask where a person wishes to die and have his or her remains buried.

Domicile can be:

- a domicile of origin, i.e. where a person was born;
- a domicile of dependence, i.e. when a child lives in different countries because his or her parents move around the world;
- a domicile of choice, i.e. when a person changes the domicile of origin by deciding to live in another country.

Once a domicile of origin has been changed, it is possible for it to be revived if a later domicile of choice is lost.

Example

Mr A is born in the USA. This is his domicile of origin. His parents are in business and move to Hong Kong when he is five years old and live there for 10 years. This becomes his domicile of dependence. His parents then move to England with Mr A who lives in England until the age of 25. This again becomes his domicile of dependence and may become his domicile of choice once he decides to live here when he is 18. Mr A returns to the USA with the intention that he will not return to England, but is unsure where he wishes to settle. He will lose his English domicile and his domicile of origin will revive. He then marries an English woman and immediately comes to live in England. The English court would be able to divorce the couple on the basis of the wife's English domicile or provided they lived in England a year, on the husband's one year residence. After a period, a domicile of choice would arise and the English court would be able to

> entertain divorce proceedings, on the basis of Mr A's domicile as well as his wife's. When Mr A retires he and his wife return to the USA and she becomes a US citizen. Mr A gives up his English domicile as he has decided not to live in England anymore and he will acquire a US domicile as he has decided to die in the USA.

The English court will not entertain divorce proceedings for people who live abroad unless one of them has English domicile. If proceedings are brought in England and Wales and also in the jurisdictions of Northern Ireland, Scotland and the Channel Islands, then the English court will decide which court is the most appropriate and 'stay' (stop) the English proceedings if appropriate.

Where two countries are able to entertain divorce proceedings then it is in the court which is the most convenient or the court in the country with which the parties have had the strongest connection (where the marital home is, where the family lived longest or had the intention of returning to) that the proceedings should take place.

The court considers the fairness and convenience for both the parties and the witnesses, and which court will proceed with the least delay; and whether under the laws of the other country, either party would be unfairly treated.

Before proceedings are commenced, where there is a choice in respect of where proceedings can be issued, it is important to consider how each of the countries will deal with matters such as the basis for the divorce and the timing. It is also important to consider what criteria are used by the different countries in determining an application for financial relief. Some countries will divide equally the matrimonial property, excluding inherited wealth, whereas others adopt a system of adjusting the assets to achieve a fair settlement between the parties, such as England. It can be appropriate to obtain legal advice in both jurisdictions, before deciding in which country to proceed.

If there is likely to be an issue between the parties as to which court system to use, it is important to issue proceedings in the chosen court first, as this will be taken into account by both courts when the issue arises as to which court should deal with the divorce.

> **Example**
>
> A German man is married to an English woman. They live in Germany for the first five years of marriage and in England for the last four years of their nine year marriage. Both German and English courts have jurisdiction. The English court is preferable for the wife (because the English court will take into account all the assets at the time of the divorce, whereas the German court may leave out any inherited property in determining the financial settlement).

Where there are two sets of divorce proceedings in different countries, the English court can stay the English proceedings if it is satisfied that the proceedings should proceed in the other country. It can also direct that one party withdraw the proceedings in the other jurisdiction.

Void/voidable marriages

Void and voidable marriages are ones which have not legally taken effect and can be set aside by nullity proceedings rather than divorce proceedings. Where a marriage is found to be void or voidable, the court can still exercise its powers in respect of financial relief. In some circumstances it will be procedurally easier to proceed on the usual grounds for a divorce if one of the facts for divorce apply.

A void marriage is one which has never taken place. Strictly speaking, no order is required as the marriage did not exist in the first place but a declaration can be sought. All cases for a declaration that a marriage is voidable by reason of mental disorder, or that the respondent had VD or was pregnant by another man at the time of the marriage, must be commenced within three years of the date of marriage. The only exception is if one party had mental illness for a period during the first three years of marriage. The period may be extended with the leave of the court.

An application that a marriage is void can be made even when one party is dead and the court has the power to make an order if either party had English domicile prior to their death or were habitually resident for the year before the death in England and Wales.

A void marriage is one where one or more of the following applies.

- The parties were within the 'prohibited degrees' (too closely related), either of the full-blood or of the half-blood. For example, a brother and sister, or half-brother and half-sister cannot marry.

- One party is under the age of 16 years or where a child is aged 16 or 17 and the parent or legal guardian has refused consent to the marriage. If the marriage is a civil marriage, the person entitled to give consent must write the word 'Forbidden' in the Superintendent Registrar's marriage notice book, and if it is in church, the person must publicly object to the marriage at the time of the calling of the banns.

- The formalities of the marriage have not been complied with. A marriage may either be a civil marriage in a Registry Office or other approved place, or in accordance with the rites of the Church of England after banns are published in church, or by common or special licence.

- One party to the marriage is already lawfully married. This is bigamy. If a party has previously entered a polygamous marriage abroad, in accordance with the law of the country where the marriage took place, even though the English court will recognise the validity of the polygamous marriage, a further marriage cannot be entered into in this country.

- The parties to the marriage are not respectively male and female.

- The parties have validly entered into a polygamous marriage under the law of another country, and one party had British domicile at the time of the marriage.

A voidable marriage is one where the parties have gone through a valid ceremony of marriage, but for other reasons the marriage can be set aside.

A voidable marriage is one where one or more of the following applies.

- The marriage has not been consummated due to the incapacity of either party (such as impotence). A person can only rely on his own failure to consummate the marriage if it is due to his inability rather than his wilful refusal.

- The respondent has wilfully refused to consummate the marriage. There is an obligation on the petitioner to try and encourage consummation. Consummation is interpreted as full intercourse. Artificial insemination is not considered to be intercourse.

- There has been no valid consent by either party to the marriage by reason of duress, mistake or unsoundness of mind or otherwise. This covers: where one party has been forced into the marriage under threat; where one party is mistaken as to the identity of the person they are marrying (i.e. it is the wrong person), or a mistake as to the nature of the ceremony (i.e. that it is a wedding); where one party is unable to understand what they were doing at the time of the marriage; where one party did not know what they were doing, for example, as a result of alcohol or drugs.

The fact that a marriage is 'arranged' for some reason other than the usual reason, such as that a spouse can acquire the right to remain in England and Wales, is not sufficient for a finding that the marriage is voidable. Where there has been an 'arranged marriage' and the wife has entered into the marriage as a result of pressure from her family, the court will not normally set the marriage aside unless she is able to show that the threats were such that she could not take an independent decision.

- Where the respondent had VD at the time of the marriage.
- Where the respondent was pregnant by a man other than the petitioner at the time of the marriage.

In these last two cases, it is necessary to show the court that the petitioner did not know and could not be expected to know that the respondent had VD or was pregnant at the time of the marriage.

The court must consider where there is an application that a marriage is voidable, whether the petitioner knowing that a marriage is voidable, has behaved so that the respondent believed that the petitioner would not seek to apply to have the marriage annulled and it would be unjust to the respondent to grant a decree.

Presumption of death

If a party believes that his or her spouse has been dead for a period of seven years, an application can be made to the court for an order that the marriage is at an end due to the presumed death of the other. If the circumstances of the disappearance of the spouse are such that evidence can be brought of the likely death of the spouse, such as by drowning, the application can be made within the seven year period. An application for a divorce on the basis of five years living apart can be made rather than wait the seven years, but this may have an adverse effect on inheritance rights. Under an order of presumed death, the wife would be a widow and possibly entitled under a will or intestacy or due a widow's pension, whereas on divorce she would be a former wife and lose benefits under a will or intestacy and, depending on the pension rules, not be entitled to any pension rights.

Judicial separation

An order of judicial separation is recognition by the court that the marriage is at an end and that one of the five facts applicable on divorce, has been proved. It does not, however, amount to a divorce and while the court can deal with the family's finances in a broadly similar way as on divorce, the parties remain legally married and cannot remarry. The procedure for a decree of judicial separation is broadly similar to that of the divorce. Unless there is any particular objection, such as a religious one, there is little point in applying for a judicial separation rather than a divorce.

The grounds for a divorce

The court must find that the marriage has irretrievably broken down on the basis of one of five facts which are set out below. If there is to be an immediate divorce then either adultery or behaviour must apply, otherwise the parties must have lived apart for a period of time.

Sometimes both the husband and the wife have grounds to divorce the other and then it is usually decided between the parties who should proceed with the petition. If not, it will be the first to file the papers with the court. It is better to agree the petition in advance of it being issued, than to risk contested proceedings.

There is an advantage in being the petitioner (the person who files the petition) as he or she has the control of the proceedings and can apply for the decree absolute earlier than the respondent can (the party against whom the divorce is sought). The petitioner can also delay applying for the decree absolute which can be to their advantage if there is delay in dealing with the financial relief proceedings.

If the divorce applied for is on the basis of two years living apart and consent, or five years living apart, then a respondent can stop the decree absolute until the finances are sorted out by filing a section 10(2) notice (an application under rule 2.45, after June 2000), which is a block to the decree absolute being made until the court is satisfied that the petitioner has made reasonable arrangements for financial relief for the respondent. This application is rare, although it can give considerable protection to a wife if there are large pension entitlements at stake and she stands to lose the widow's pension and other benefits on divorce.

The facts on which the petition can be based are given below.

Adultery

The respondent has committed adultery with another person and the petitioner finds it intolerable to live with him or her. The petitioner cannot rely on an incident of adultery if she or he has lived with their husband or wife for six months or more after becoming aware of the adultery. It is not necessary to know the identity of the other party and if it is known, it is not necessary to name the person in the petition. If a person is named in a petition he or she is called a 'co-respondent', and if adultery is alleged in a cross-petition, the other person is called the 'party cited'. Where a person is named in a petition, the divorce papers are served on that person and they can be asked to pay the costs of the divorce, although it is usual for the respondent to agree to pay them. It is now usual not to name a co-respondent in a petition as it is likely to cause unnecessary animosity between the parties, and it can cause considerable embarrassment to the co-respondent if he or she is still married and there can be religious implications.

Sometimes a confession statement is obtained from the respondent before the petition is issued, but this is not strictly necessary as the respondent must sign the Acknowledgement of Service personally to admit the adultery in any case.

Specimen Example for the Petition

The respondent has committed adultery and the petitioner finds it intolerable to live with the respondent.

PARTICULARS

On various dates, the last being (a date within six months), at various places including (address), the respondent has committed adultery with a woman whose name, address and identity the petitioner knows but does not wish to disclose in this petition.

Behaviour

The respondent has behaved in such a way that the petitioner cannot reasonably be expected to live with the respondent. This includes both physical violence and other behaviour, such as mental abuse, intimidation, neglect and failing to socialise together. Again, the parties must not have lived together in the same household for six months after the last incident of behaviour. The word 'same household' does not mean they cannot live at the same address, just that they must live separate lives, separate bedrooms, separate cooking, eating, socialising, etc.

It is accepted as good practice to try and agree the allegations of behaviour before the petition is issued with the spouse or their solicitor. It is quite usual to submit the draft petition for agreement before it is issued, with a view to avoiding defended proceedings.

Specimen Example for the Petition

The respondent has behaved in such a way that the petitioner cannot reasonably be expected to live with the respondent.

PARTICULARS

1 Throughout the marriage the respondent was selfish and inconsiderate to the petitioner and took little or no account of the petitioner's feeling. He used verbal abuse towards her.

2 The respondent drank alcohol to excess for the five years preceding the presentation of this petition and when under the influence would insult the petitioner and seek to embarrass her.

3 On the 25th day of December 1998 the respondent did not return home until 2.00 p.m. knowing that the petitioner's family were coming to Christmas lunch at 12.00 noon causing the petitioner considerable embarrassment. The respondent was drunk and then physically assaulted the petitioner in the presence of her visitors, causing her considerable pain and anguish.

4 On the 2nd January 1999 the petitioner left the former matrimonial home, since when the petitioner and respondent have not lived together.

5 The respondent works long hours and puts his job and career before the needs of the petitioner. He returns home at 11.00 p.m. most nights, knowing that this causes distress to the petitioner.

Desertion

The respondent has left the petitioner for a period of at least two years without just cause and the petitioner did not agree to the respondent leaving at the time of the departure or subsequently.

Where a respondent leaves without due reason and then acquires a good reason for not returning such as learning of the petitioner's adultery, it is deemed reasonable, for the respondent not to return to live with the petitioner and the petitioner cannot then rely on desertion. Where the respondent leaves for good reason such as to work abroad, and decides without good reason not to return, from the time the decision not to return is communicated to the spouse, desertion arises. It is important that the petitioner does not agree to the separation – where parties agree to live apart pending a divorce, desertion does not apply.

Specimen Example for the Petition

The respondent has deserted the petitioner for a continuous period of at least two years immediately preceding the presentation of this petition.

PARTICULARS

On the 5th June 1997 the respondent left the petitioner without just cause and without her consent with the intention of bringing co-habitation between the parties to an end permanently. He has not since returned to live with her.

Two years living apart with consent

The parties must have lived apart for two years immediately preceding the presentation of the petition. A period of up to six months living together for the purpose of a reconciliation is permitted and this period is added to the two year period. Reference to the period(s) living together should be included in the petition. Living apart can include living at the same address but the parties must have led separate lives, occupied separate bedrooms, eaten separately and each must do their own washing, cleaning and cooking. The court will require details of the addresses where the parties have lived and will need to be satisfied that the parties have lived separately. The court can require an affidavit (sworn statement) setting out the living arrangements in detail.

The respondent must consent to the divorce on the basis of two years living apart, usually by him or his solicitor signing the Acknowledgement of Service confirming this. The consent can be withdrawn up to the decree nisi being granted.

If the parties are unable to be rehoused during the two year period and have to live under the same roof, particularly where there are children, it can be extremely difficult for the parties.

Specimen Example for the Petition

The parties have lived together for a continuous period of two years immediately preceding the presentation of this petition and the respondent consents to the decree being granted.

PARTICULARS

The petitioner and respondent have lived apart since the 3rd June 1997 when the petitioner left the matrimonial home at ____.

Five years living apart

The parties have lived apart for five years immediately preceding the presentation of the petition and again a period of up to six months co-habitation during that period is permitted, provided that period is added to the five year period. No consent is required and it is possible for both parties including the person who left the marital home to file the petition on the basis of the separation. This is the appropriate basis on which a person who has committed a matrimonial offence to proceed where their spouse refuses to bring divorce proceedings.

Where there is a petition on this basis, the respondent is able to oppose the grant of the decree on the basis that it will cause 'grave financial hardship' or other hardship to the respondent. The court can refuse to dissolve the marriage if it considers this would be wrong in all the circumstances. Financial hardship would include a situation where the respondent will suffer financially because of the divorce. For example, where there are significant widow's pension rights which the respondent would lose on divorce and for which she cannot be compensated in other ways. Other hardship can include religious objections to divorce, or because a person will be ostracised by their community if they are divorced.

Specimen Example for the Petition

The parties have lived apart for a continuous period of five years immediately preceding the presentation of this petition.

The petitioner and respondent have live apart since the 5th June 1994 when the respondent left the matrimonial home at ___ since which date the parties have not resumed co-habitation.

The divorce process

This section deals with the technical process of the divorce and includes details of the court papers which need to be completed and filed with the court in order to progress. The procedure laid out applies to all divorces in England and Wales at the present time. As a result of new trials taking place in the country there may be additional steps which need to be complied with according to the rules of each court and if one of the parties to the marriage is seeking legal aid it may be necessary to attend a 'section 29 meeting' (see page 169). No petition may be filed until a year has passed since the date of marriage.

Which court?

Divorce proceedings are conducted by the county court, which is the lowest of the civil courts. Proceedings can be brought in any county court in the county which has divorce jurisdiction.

The main divorce court for London is the Principal Registry of the Family Division (see page 182 for the address). The judges there deal solely with family matters, whereas judges in county courts generally hear cases which are both matrimonial and non-matrimonial.

There are two tiers of judges in the county court, namely the district judge (previously called the Registrar) who deals with the divorce petition and the making of the decree nisi. District judges also deal with the procedural stages of the financial relief application and any dispute concerning children. If a matter is contested, then either a district judge will hear the case or, if there are special circumstances such as complex issues to determine on finance, it can be transferred to a circuit judge to decide. Where a matter is very complex or raises difficult legal issues, it may be heard by a High Court judge.

The consideration of which court to bring proceedings in usually depends on the convenience of the parties and to a lesser extent the convenience of the legal advisers representing the parties. There can be advantages in bringing cases in the Principal Registry if a matter is complex or the family is wealthy as the judges have greater experience in hearing such cases.

If the case involves people in the public eye and they wish to avoid publicity, there can be advantages in proceeding in an appropriate county court rather than the Principal Registry. The hearing of a contested divorce is in public, i.e. the general public can attend. In uncontested proceedings the list of cases where a decree nisi are to be granted is published and journalists scrutinise the court list for famous people. In financial matters, the proceedings are in private so that members of the public are not allowed to be present in court or see the court papers. Children's cases are highly confidential and save in exceptional circumstances where a judge orders it, the identity of the children may not be disclosed.

The petition

The 'divorce petition' is the court document which sets out the history of the marriage and why the petitioner wants a divorce. Blank forms are available from law stationers (see page 182) and the court.

The information required to complete the petition is as follows:

- The full names of the petitioner (the person who files the divorce petition) and respondent (the person on whom the petition is served) as they appear in the marriage certificate. The name of the wife can be given in her married name with her maiden name given in brackets. If either party has changed their name, both names should be included.

- The date and place where the marriage took place (again as they appear in the marriage certificate). If there is more than one marriage ceremony, reference to both should be included.

■ The occupation of both parties. If one party does not work, ascertain how they describe themselves, for example housewife, mother, unemployed, retired. The description may seem unimportant, but can cause offence to the person. It can also be relevant to the financial relief application. For example, if a person worked as a secretary 15 years ago and then stopped to raise a family, if the description given in the petition is 'secretary', a judge on a financial relief application is more inclined to treat the person as being employable as a secretary, whereas if the description is 'housewife', the judge will consider whether the person is employable.

■ The last address where the parties lived together as husband and wife.

■ If the marriage is polygamous (i.e there is more than one wife), this fact should be stated and details of any living spouses additional to the respondent should be given.

■ The present address of both parties. In some circumstances, for example, where a petitioner fears violence if the respondent knew where to find her, an application can be made for leave to omit the petitioner's address from the petition. The court will require that the address is provided to the court for the court's records.

■ Details of all 'children of the family'. A child of the family is a child of both husband and wife or a child of either party, if treated by both parties as a child of the family (see page 134). The full names and dates of birth of all such children under the age of 18 must be included. If a child is between 16 and 18 years old, a statement should be included if the child is in full-time education which includes school, university and vocational training. The full names of all children of the family aged 18 and over should be given, including a statement that they are over the age of 18 years and whether they are in full-time education.

- Details of any living child born to the wife during the marriage who is not the child of the husband. If it is disputed whether a child is a child of the family, this should be stated.
- Details of any special needs affecting any child who is over the age of 18, such as a mental handicap.
- Details of any previous legal proceedings either in England and Wales or elsewhere in the world, dealing with the marriage or any property belonging to the parties. Details of the case name, action number, court and address should be included. The outcome of the proceedings and if the proceeding related to the legal status of the marriage, whether co-habitation has resumed subsequently.
- Details of any other existing proceedings in England and Wales and elsewhere in the world. Details of the action number, the type of proceedings, the name and address of the court, the action number of the proceedings, details of the orders that have been made and the date of any final hearing should be included.
- Information on whether there has been an application for an assessment under the Child Support Act 1991, and if so, the date of the application and details of any assessment made.
- If the petition is on the basis of five years living apart, a statement whether there is any agreement for the support of the respondent and any child of the family. If there is an agreement or a proposal as to the financial arrangements, these should be set out in the petition.
- A statement that the 'marriage has irretrievably broken down' and the fact(s) relied upon. Details should be included in respect of the various facts (see page 28).
- The address of the petitioner and his or her solicitor if there are solicitors, and the address of the respondent and his or her solicitor if the papers are to be served on the respondent's solicitor.

■ Where it is an adultery petition and it is intended to name the co-respondent, the person's name and address and if they have solicitors, the solicitors' details so that the petition can be served on them.

■ If the respondent has been found guilty of any offence, found to have committed adultery in other proceedings or found to have fathered a child, a statement to that effect must be included.

Specimen Divorce Petition

IN THE PRINCIPAL REGISTRY/ County Court _____ CASE NO _____ of 2000

THE PETITION of _____ SHOWS THAT:

1 On the _____ day of _____ 20 __, the Petitioner _____ was lawfully married to _____ (hereinafter called 'the respondent') at the _____ in the County of _____.

2 The Petitioner and the Respondent have lived together as husband and wife at _____.

3 The Petitioner is domiciled in England and Wales and the Respondent is domiciled in England and Wales.

4 The Petitioner is by occupation a _____ and resides at _____ and the Respondent is by occupation a _____ and resides at _____.

5 There are _____ children of the family namely _____ who was born on the _____.

6 No other child now living has been Petitioner during the marriage except _____.

7 There have been no previous proceedings in any court in England and Wales or elsewhere with reference to the said marriage (or to any child of the family) or between the Petitioner and Respondent with reference to any property of either or both of them save that _____.

8 There has (not) been an application under the Child Support Act 1991 for a maintenance assessment in respect of the children of the family.

9   There are no proceedings continuing in any country outside England and Wales which are in respect of the marriage or are capable of affecting its validity or subsistence except _____.

10 *5 year separation only.* No agreement or arrangement has been made (is proposed to be made between the parties for the support of the parties (or the said children) except _____.

11 The said marriage has broken down irretrievably.

The Respondent has (set out the ground for the divorce, see individual sections above).

PARTICULARS

12 (Set out the basis of the divorce – see individual sections above)

THE PETITIONER THEREFORE PRAYS:

1 That the said marriage may be dissolved.

2 That the respondent (and the co-respondent) may be ordered to pay the costs of this suit.

3 That the petitioner may be granted an order under the Children Act 1989 namely a residence (contact) order in respect of the said children.

4 That the petitioner may be granted the following relief:

   (a)   order for maintenance pending suit;

   (b)   a periodical payments order;

   (c)   a secured provision order;

   (d)   a lump sum order;

   (e)   a periodical payments order for the children of the family;

   (f)   a secured provision order for the children of the family;

   (g)   a property adjustment order in respect of _____;

   (h)   pension provision namely _____.

Signature _____

The names and address(es) of the person(s) who are to be served with this petition are _____ of _____ .

The Petitioner's address for service is c/o _____.

The Statement of Arrangement for Children: Form M4

This document must be filed with the petition if there are any children of the family under the age of 16, or between the age of 16 and 18 and receiving full-time education or training. It should include details of step-children and adopted children who are treated by both parents as a child of the family. The document sets out details of the existing accommodation, the existing arrangements for the children, and any changes there will be. It sets out the petitioner's proposals for the children including with whom they are to live on the divorce and the arrangements for them to see the other parent.

It is preferable if the other parent can agree the arrangements and it is good practice to give the other parent the proposed statement of arrangement and invite him or her to sign it, before the petition is issued. The petitioner is able to indicate whether he or she will agree to conciliation if there is a disagreement over contact.

The court considers the arrangements for the children when making the decree nisi (see pages 43, 142).

Papers to file with the court

The following need to be filed with the relevant court:

- Divorce petition with a copy for the court. If there is a named co-respondent a further copy is required. A copy should be retained for own use.
- Statement of Arrangement for Children, together with a copy. A copy should be retained for own use.
- Original marriage certificate. If it is not in English, an English translation is required.
- If a solicitor is instructed, he or she needs to file a 'certificate with regard to reconciliation', confirming whether the solicitor has discussed reconciliation and whether he or she has given contact numbers of a conciliator.
- Legal aid certificate, if legal aid is available, and a copy of the Notice of Issue of legal aid. Usually full legal aid

is not available for a divorce although legal aid is available under the Green Form Scheme.

■ Court fee, currently £150, or 'Fees Exemption Application' if the petitioner is in receipt of income support or family credit.

The court will issue the petition and send it by post to the respondent together with the Acknowledgement of Service and Notes in Support. If there are relevant children the Statement of Arrangement for Children will be sent as well.

If a solicitor's address is included in the divorce petition, the papers are sent to the solicitor. Alternatively, if preferred, the divorce petition can be issued by the court, and collected and served by the petitioner or the lawyer. A petitioner is not allowed personally to 'serve' (give) the divorce papers on the respondent.

Acknowledgement of Service

The respondent has eight days to file the Acknowledgement of Service with the court, although this time limit is not strictly complied with.

The details required are the date and place the document was received by the respondent, whether he or she agrees the allegations, whether he or she accepts the request for costs on the petition, whether he or she agrees the Statement of Arrangement for Children, if applicable, whether the marriage is polygamous. If the respondent intends defending the petition he or she must state so in the Acknowledgement of Service.

Where the petition is served on the basis of adultery and the respondent is admitting the adultery, he or she must sign the Acknowledgement of Service, together with the solicitor if there is one. Where there are petitions based on other facts, the solicitor can sign it on his or her client's behalf.

If the respondent wishes to defend the petition he or she should state on the form that he or she objects to the petition and in those circumstances should comply with the eight day time limit. He or she will then need to file an 'answer' (defence) within 29 days of the date of receipt of the petition (see page 46).

If the respondent does not agree the arrangements for the children he or she can file his own Statement of Arrangement for children, setting out his or her proposals.

It is courteous to provide a copy of the Acknowledgement of Service to the other party or their lawyer, when it is filed with the court as this can avoid delays in the acknowledgement being forwarded by the court.

If the Acknowledgement of Service is not returned to the court by the respondent, it may be necessary to obtain a further copy of the divorce petition and court papers and arrange for personal service on the respondent. A process server can be employed to effect service. He or she will require a photograph and description of the respondent and an address where he or she will be. He or she will prepare an affidavit of service once the papers have been served confirming the date and place where the papers were served. Alternatively the court bailiff can serve the papers personally.

Sometimes the address and whereabouts of the respondent are not known to the petitioner, for example if it is a petition for desertion or five years living apart. In this situation the court can be asked to give leave for either substituted service (i.e. when the papers are not served on the respondent and an advertisement is placed in a suitable newspaper) or for service to be dispensed with (i.e. when the papers do not need to be served on the respondent at all.)

Directions for trial

Once the Acknowledgement of Service is filed with the court (or if the question of service has been dealt with as above), an affidavit in support of the petition is prepared (using the prescribed Form M7 – a) to e) depending on the basis of the petition) and sworn by the petitioner, and filed with the court with the 'Application for Directions for Trial'. It is good practice to notify the respondent that the application has been filed with the court.

There are different affidavits for the different grounds of the petition. The purpose of the affidavit is to confirm the truth of the petition. Amendments can be made to the petition in the affidavit, for example, if it has been agreed not to seek an order for costs or where an example of behaviour is to be withdrawn.

Where the petition is based on periods living apart, the addresses at which the petitioner and respondent have lived must be included. Where it is a behaviour petition the petitioner can state whether the behaviour has effected his or her health and medical evidence can be exhibited (attached to the affidavit).

The Acknowledgement of Service, if signed by the respondent personally and any Statement of Arrangement for Children signed by the respondent should be exhibited and the signature identified as the respondent's.

Decree nisi

After the application and affidavit in support are filed with the court there is a delay of some six to eight weeks, depending on the court while the district judge considers the papers and, if he or she is satisfied that the petitioner has sufficient grounds for a divorce, will make an order and give the date for the decree nisi.

The district judge can seek clarification on any point. Most commonly, if the petition is on the basis of two years living apart with consent and the parties have continued to live in the same property, the district judge may want further details about the living arrangements and will want to be satisfied that the parties have been living separately.

The judge at the same time is obliged to make a statement that there are or are not children to whom Matrimonial Causes Act 1973 section 41 applies. See page 142 where the court's options are discussed.

If there is an issue which is not agreed, such as the costs, the district judge can give 'directions' (instructions) how it is to be dealt with.

The notice of decree nisi is issued by the court and will show the basis of the divorce, the date of the decree nisi (which is usually within about two weeks of the notification) and the position with regard to the children. The usual order where children are involved is that 'there are children to whom section 41 applies and the court is satisfied with the arrangements made'. Neither the parties, nor their solicitors, normally attend the decree nisi appointment.

If a financial consent order has been agreed and filed with the application for the decree nisi, the financial order can be made at the same time as the decree nisi. (See page 88).

Decree absolute

It is only once the decree absolute has been granted that the parties cease to be husband and wife and can remarry. Six weeks after the decree nisi is granted, the decree absolute can be given, if the petitioner applies for it.

Example

If, for example the decree nisi is given on Wednesday, 1st September, the application for the decree nisi to be made absolute can be made on Thursday 14th October.

The application for decree absolute is made on Form M8 and is lodged with the court fee. The decree absolute with a red court seal is issued within two of days of the application and a copy is sent to the husband and wife. The document should be kept safely as it will be needed if either wish to remarry.

If the petitioner does not apply for decree absolute, the respondent has to wait a further three months from the date the petitioner can apply and must apply to the court for permission. A hearing takes place and the court will decide whether the respondent can be granted the decree absolute. The reason for refusing the decree absolute would be that the petitioner would suffer a financial loss such as the loss of pension rights, and the decree would have to wait until the financial aspect is resolved.

The effect of the decree absolute is as follows.

■ Any appointment of the other spouse or gift to them in a will, will be cancelled.

■ The spouse will no longer be able to inherit as a widow, if there is an intestacy.

■ The wife will no longer be a widow and will not be entitled to a widow's benefit.

■ The widow will not be entitled to the state's widow's benefit.

■ Any right of occupation under the Matrimonial Homes Act will cease, unless the court has ordered otherwise, before the decree absolute.

Frequently, where the financial aspect has not been agreed, the decree absolute will be delayed until the finances are agreed. A husband/wife should delay applying for the decree absolute until his/her financial provision has been agreed or determined.

If the divorce is on the basis of five years living apart, the court may refuse to grant the decree nisi if to do so would cause the respondent 'grave financial or other hardship and it would be wrong in all the circumstances to dissolve the marriage'.

If the respondent to the divorce (on the basis of two years living apart with consent or five years separation) wishes to prevent the decree absolute until after the financial settlement is in place, he or she can block the decree absolute by filing an application under Matrimonial Causes Act 1973 section 10(2) (using the prescribed Form M12 or after June 2000 Form B) within the six week period after decree nisi, or at least before the decree absolute is granted. The decree absolute will then only be made by the court once it is satisfied that the financial relief which has been made for the respondent is reasonable. This differs in wording, but not effect, from the usual financial relief application. It can be a powerful weapon, if the petitioner is anxious for a speedy decree absolute although it is not often used as a procedure.

There can be situations where one party wants the decree absolute as a matter of urgency, frequently so that he or she can remarry quickly where a child is about to be born. An application can be made on the decree nisi for an expedited order setting out the reasons for the urgency.

If there is a delay of a year after the grant of decree nisi for applying for the decree absolute, the court must be satisfied:

■ whether the parties have lived together since the decree nisi and, if so, the dates;

■ that no child has been born to the wife, if she is the petitioner, or whether a child has been born to the wife so far as the petitioner knows, if the husband is the petitioner.

A letter satisfying these points can be filed with the application for the decree absolute. If the delay has been occasioned by sorting out the finance, the court can give leave for the decree absolute at the time of dealing with the financial application. Sometimes the judge will require the petitioner to set out the facts in an affidavit.

Very rarely, an application can be made, either by some third party, or the Queen's Proctor (an official) to the court to show that there are material factors which the court was not aware of, which would justify the court not making the decree nisi absolute. The court has the power to:

- make the decree absolute;
- rescind (cancel) the decree;
- ask for further information;
- deal with the matter as it wishes.

The defended case

Where a party wishes to defend a petition, he or she must file 'an answer' (a written document stating what the objections are to the petition) with the court within 21 days after the time limit for giving notice of intention to defend, i.e. filing the Acknowledgement of Service indicating that the petition will be defended. If he or she fails to lodge the answer within the time limit and the petitioner applies for the decree nisi, an application can be made for the period to file the answer to be extended, but the court is usually unsympathetic to such an application.

The answer should 'admit' (agree) facts that are accepted, and should 'dispute' (object to) the facts in the petition which are untrue. If facts are admitted which would entitle the petitioner to a decree, the court will allow the petition to proceed on the limited uncontested facts. If there is a claim for financial relief, this should be set out in detail in the answer, as it is in the divorce petition.

In addition to defending the petition, the answer can include a 'cross-prayer' (request a divorce against the petitioner). The cross-petition has the same standing as a divorce petition and should set out the basis on which a divorce is sought against the petitioner using the same grounds as in a petition (see page 28). It may include a 'prayer' (request) for a nullity.

The petitioner can file a 'reply to an answer' within 14 days of receiving the answer and this again sets out the objections to the facts set out in the cross-petition in the same way as the cross-petition objects to the facts set out in the petition. If no reply is filed, it is accepted by the court that the petitioner does not accept the facts as set out in the reply.

Once an answer is filed with the court, the case is treated as a defended cause and will be referred to the High Court if the matter is complex or the issues grave or difficult, rather than the county court for the hearing, although this makes little practical difference. The petitioner should file, 'a request for directions for trial' with the court and the court will give a date for a directions hearing when the court decides the length of the hearing, where it should take place, and any other directions including any documents which must be disclosed.

The final hearing date will then be set and a hearing will take place when both parties will be able to present their cases to the court.

The court will try and encourage the parties to agree to a divorce proceeding undefended, but if a way cannot be found to allow the petition to proceed or to allow decrees on the petition and cross-petition, there will be a hearing. Fully contested proceedings are extremely rare and usually a divorce is granted.

Frequently, a compromise can be agreed and a consent order signed by both parties, setting out whether the petition or cross petition will be withdrawn. The decision to allow the matter to proceed undefended can be filed with the court, and the matter can proceed uncontested (see page 42).

If, after the original petition is filed, there are further incidents on which to base the petition, then a 'supplemental petition' may be filed and the court's 'leave' (permission) will be required before it is filed. Alternatively, if after the original petition was filed, a new ground for a divorce applies such as that the parties have lived apart for two years, then 'a second petition' may be filed and again leave of the court is required.

The new law

In 1996 a new divorce law was approved which provided that the requirement for grounds for the divorce should be removed, and introduced divorce over time, on the basis that as part of the process the parties should be given information on the consequences of divorce and encouragement from mediators and counsellors to try and save the marriage.

Since then, trials have been run in order to ensure the smooth-running of procedures and it was expected that the new law would be in place in the year 2000. The government, however, said in June 1999 that although it remains committed to the new law, the implementation has been delayed indefinitely. A further announcement about the future of the act is due in the summer of 2000.

The intention is that at an information meeting, which the parties have the right to attend jointly or separately, they will be given information about the alternative courses available, with an emphasis on mediation and effecting a reconciliation.

Procedure

Day 1	Attend information meeting. Commencement of three months cooling off period.
3 months	File 'Statement of Marital Breakdown' – this is the commencement of the divorce process.
3 months 2 weeks	Service of the 'Statement of Marital Breakdown' and the period of reflection and consideration commences. This period differs according to circumstances; namely
9 months	Period of reflection and consideration if no children, or children over 16 years.
or 15 months	Extension to period of reflection and consideration if children under 16 or where either party applies for more time for further reflection.

This takes the period from commencement to either 12 months 2 weeks or 18 months 2 weeks.

next 12 months	Within the period, file application for final order provided all matters are concluded (e.g. finance, children).

This takes the period from commencement to 24 months 2 weeks for couples without children and 30 months 2 weeks for families with children under 16 as above.

There will be a delay between applying for final order and the making of final order, expected to be about four weeks.

Reduction in time

It will be possible to mitigate the six months extension to the period of reflection and consideration where there are children under 16 years namely:

- where there is an occupation order in force (similar to an ouster order) or a non-molestation order in favour of the party applying for divorce or a child of the family;
- where the court is satisfied that to delay the order would be significantly detrimental to the welfare of any child of the family.

Extra time

The spouses will be able to live together throughout the period and can 'stop the clock' from running by giving notice that they are attempting a reconciliation. Time starts again when either party gives notice that the reconciliation has been unsuccessful. The maximum extra time allowed is 18 months.

Knock out

If time stops running for 18 months (see under Extra time above), then the process stops and goes back to Day 1. The separation or divorce order will only be made if, in addition to the period of time and steps required by the Act have been complied with, the parties have arranged finance and all other matters resulting from the divorce within the further 12 month period (or as extended above). If arrangements are not in place, then no order, and, process goes back to Day 1.

So for a couple with children under 16, the maximum time to sort out all aspects is four years.

Legal aid cases

See section on legal aid on page 169.

3 | THE FINANCIAL CLAIM

In this chapter the financial claim is discussed, definitions of the technical terms provided, and the procedure used to make a financial claim and the different types of settlements are explained. Two different procedures are explained: the original procedure and the Pilot Scheme. In June 2000 the Pilot Scheme will be implemented nationwide with certain amendments. These are set out on page 174.

Definition of financial claims

As soon as divorce proceedings are commenced the court can deal with the financial arrangements between the parties. The court deals with finances, both capital and income, by seeking to impose a reasonable settlement on the basis of a number of factors. It is not a mathematical division of the assets or an attempt to equalise the assets that have been generated while the parties have been married.

The court requires both parties to give full and frank disclosure of their means up to the date of the hearing and it will determine the matter on the basis of the facts as they are at the time of the hearing.

> **Example**
> Husband and wife separate in 1990 when property prices depressed. Matrimonial home then worth £150,000. Divorce 1995. Financial application dealt with by the court in 1998. Matrimonial home current value £300,000. Court takes value at £300,000 for the purpose of determining the case.

Both husband and wife are entitled to make financial claims against the other, although in practice it is usually the wife who makes a claim against a husband. The court should deal with the matter irrespective of the gender of the parties and accordingly the husband can make a claim. If he is the weaker party financially, for example, through illness, an order can be made in his favour. For the purpose of this part, the presumption is that the wife is the weaker party financially.

The different financial claims are explained below.

Maintenance pending suit

This deals with the living costs until the decree nisi is granted. It covers the interim financial provision up to the making of the final financial order.

An application can be made after the petition is issued for the court to provide for her (and any children's) immediate needs, prior to the full enquiry taking place. Usually the *status quo* is maintained so that if, for example, the husband has previously paid the mortgage and given the wife £1,000 per month to pay her living costs, this should continue. Because of the increased costs of maintaining two properties, the basic needs should be met, but not matters in respect of luxuries.

Applications are usually avoided by the husband agreeing to continue making voluntary payments to the wife. The application will be dealt with by the court in the same way as a full application for financial relief, although the opportunity to ask questions about the financial position of the other will be far more limited and the court has to decide the case without necessarily a full financial enquiry taking place. If the maintenance provision is intended to cover the period after the decree nisi, it will be described as 'interim periodical payments'.

Periodical payments

Periodical payments are the regular payments made by one party to the other to cover living expenses. They are usually made monthly. Unless the order states otherwise, they will be paid 'in arrear', i.e. at month end for the previous month (like a salary). It is better to provide that the payments are to be made 'in advance' so that they cover the expenses of the following month. An undertaking can be included for the payments to be made by standing order to the recipient's bank account. A periodical payments order can be varied by the court in the future if the circumstances of one or other party has changed. In order to avoid the need for such an application (or reduce the likelihood of such a need), the periodical payments sum can be index-linked, for example, by reference to the Retail Price Index.

Secured periodical payments order

'Secured provision' means that the liability for periodical payments is secured against some asset, frequently a property, to ensure that the periodical payments will be made. If the payments have been made the secured asset is released when the liability has been met, such as a child completing education. In the event that the periodical payments are not paid, the asset is sold and the proceeds used to meet the periodical payments. This type of order is not usual but is helpful where the paying party has capital assets and is not in employment, or is likely to disappear.

Lump sum order

A 'lump sum order' is an order for a capital sum of money to be paid. The lump sum will be determined by reference to the overall financial position of the parties and can be designed to meet a housing need, cover debts or compensate one party for the loss of other rights that they will lose on divorce, such as pension rights. A lump sum order can be paid as one payment or by instalments. It can be payable at a future time, or when a future event occurs. Where it is payable at a future date, an application can be made to vary the time for payment of the lump sum. Where there are substantial assets, it may be possible for a lump sum to be paid, out of which the recipient can meet her future living needs rather than periodical payments being paid. See 'clean break', page 97.

Until 1998, only one lump sum order could be made on a divorce. As a result of changes then, the court now has the power to grant a further lump sum. This power is available only where a capital payment is made to buy out an existing maintenance obligation. This will apply where, after the original order, the paying party's financial position has changed to the extent that he can pay the wife a lump sum rather than maintenance payments.

Interest can be ordered to be paid from the date of the order to the date the payment is ordered to be made. If the payment is over

£5,000, interest is payable under the High Court rules. If it is less then £5,000, a specific provision in the order is required for interest.

Since the introduction of 'earmarking orders' in respect of lump sums payable out of retirement pensions (see page 117), the court has power to order the pension trustees to make the payment out of the pension fund, on behalf of the pension holder. Lump sum orders may also be made in favour of a child. The court does not have the power to order an 'interim lump sum', i.e. a lump sum on account of the final financial order to provide for housing for one party.

Property adjustment orders

A property adjustment order applies where the court orders the transfer of an asset, usually a property, to the other party. Where a wife, for example, wants a property in which the spouse has an interest transferred to herself, she must include a specific claim for the property, (which should be included in the divorce petition, if the party is the petitioner, and in the financial application). The property should be identified by its address and, if registered at the Land Registry, the land registration number. (This can be obtained by doing an index map search at the Land Registry.) If there is a mortgagee, details should be included in the application and the building society or bank must be notified of the application and given 14 days notice to respond (see page 58).

Pension

Under present law, a party can apply for an order whereby part of the pension entitlement of the spouse is 'earmarked', i.e. allocated to that party. The benefit is still treated as belonging to the spouse and will only be paid when the spouse retires and claims his benefit. It is treated as the spouse's so that there is no tax advantage at present. The pension in this context includes a retirement pension (but not the state pension). The advantage is that the pension trustees can make the payment direct to the party so that there is some certainty that the payments will be made (see page 115 for more detail). There are changes due at the end of 2000 which will introduce 'pension sharing' see page 178.

Matters the court takes into account

The court takes into account a number of factors that are set out in the legislation, known as 'section 25 criteria' in determining what is a fair settlement. It is for the judge to decide the importance to be given to each factor in each individual case and to balance the various factors. There is usually a bracket within which the court will determine a case and the judge determines within that framework whether to be more generous or not. A judge will decide whether he accepts the evidence of the parties. The factors taken into account are given below.

History of marriage

The length of marriage is relevant. If it is a short childless marriage, i.e. one or two years, the court will try and put the parties back in the situation they were before the marriage.

> **Example**
> A young couple marry, the marriage lasts one year, and both husband and wife continue in their respective employment. The wife was in a rented flat before the marriage and moved into the husband's house which he had bought prior to the marriage. The husband has £10,000 in assets. The court would give the wife a small capital payment of £5,000 to assist her in getting a new flat.

The ages of the parties is also relevant. Where there is a young childless couple it is easy to create a final division between them. Where the parties are older, there are other considerations such as how soon will they retire and what the position will be after retirement. Age has an effect on employment prospects (see page 56).

The behaviour of one party to the other is relevant, as it forms part of the history of the marriage. Where one party has behaved in such a way to the other that 'it would be inequitable to disregard it', the court can take such behaviour into account in order to give an enhanced award. The behaviour can be both financial, i.e. hiding assets, or non-financial such as mental abuse. It does not apply to simple situations of marriage breakdown such as adultery or domestic violence. The behaviour must be such that the recipient's ability to look after herself financially has been effected.

> **Example**
>
> Contrast the position of the non-working wife who has suffered post-traumatic shock syndrome as a result of the husband's violence towards her, and the career woman, suffering similarly to the extent that she is no longer able to work. In the first case, there is no financial loss as the first wife was fully dependent and as she would be fully provided for anyhow, there will be no difference to the award. In the second case, the wife has lost her financial independence as a result of the husband's behaviour and she should be compensated for the loss of her financial independence as well as provided for to meet her needs.

Where it is a long marriage, for example, seven years and over, the court will fully compensate the wife for her financial and non-financial contribution, which includes looking after children. The court will need also to take into account pension benefits which have accrued over a long marriage.

Contribution

The court must have regard to the financial and non-financial contribution made by the parties. This includes the property and other financial resources each party has or is likely to have in the foreseeable future. Non-financial contribution includes looking after the home and children. The court will pay regard to assets brought into the marriage by one or other party and the source of monies generated during the marriage is relevant, including the monies that have come from inheritance. Future resources includes inheritances and interests in trusts.

Needs

The court takes into account the standard of living enjoyed during the marriage. It will be the court's aim to place both parties in a similar position to that enjoyed during the marriage, although this is no longer an overriding consideration. This is usually difficult as the money that maintained one unit will have to meet two units. The court seeks to ensure that both the husband and wife have adequate funds to provide for their respective housing needs.

'Needs' includes a maintenance need, particularly of a non-working mother with children. The needs of the children are always paramount, i.e. the most important factor to be taken in to account (see page 57 under 'Children').

'Needs' covers special needs such as additional requirements brought on by illness or incapacity of a spouse or a child of the family and is interpreted as providing reasonable housing and sufficient maintenance. In many cases there are insufficient means to provide adequately for both spouses and their separate households. In those circumstances it will be the parent with whom the children do not live who will receive substantially less. Sometimes, in the light of state benefit, the mother will keep the former matrimonial home and then receive no other financial assistance from the husband relying on state benefit to pay the mortgage.

Employment prospects

The court must have regard to the income of any working party or the earning capacity (income they could earn) of a non-working spouse and any increase in this capacity which it would be reasonable to expect.

Usually the man is in employment and his income will be a regular amount each week/month. Where a person has variable overtime, or a variable income, an average is taken over a reasonable period. If there are bonuses paid on an *ad-hoc* basis, regard will be given as to how likely the bonus is to be paid again. In assessing a person's income, the tax, national insurance, cost of travel to and from work and any other costs associated with the work are taken into account, as well as any perks or benefits, such as the provision of a company car, accommodation, share option schemes, pension benefits.

Where a person, usually a wife, is not working because she has stopped to have children, her earning capacity is taken into account. A court will take a realistic attitude to a wife's prospects of employment when she is the prime carer for young children. When the children are young, in many cases it is not economically viable for the wife to work because of the cost of child care. A woman will frequently be expected to be able to obtain some part-time employment when the children attend full-time education, but such earnings after allowing for child care are frequently quite low. If a wife has children at school who are not yet eleven years of age, a court is unlikely to expect the wife to work full-time. When the children are over eleven the court may consider that a wife should obtain employment, but it has to take a realistic view of the wife's previous work experience, her qualifications, skills the likelihood of her obtaining employment and the type of salary she will command. The court will take into account the need for a person who is out of employment for a period of time to undergo some retraining.

Children

The court must determine all cases where there are children to protect their interests. The main need for the children is housing, and it is usual for the parent with whom they live to have sufficient accommodation for them, even if this means that the other parent has very modest accommodation. It is accepted that if possible, each child should have their own bedroom. If it is possible, the children should remain in the former matrimonial home with, usually, their mother. If this cannot be afforded, the best alternative is for the children to be moved into a smaller and more modest property, in the same locality, so that they have the same friends and their schools are unchanged. Until the Child Support Act 1991, the court had to deal with child maintenance, called periodical payments. The effect of this Act is that child maintenance can be dealt with by means of an assessment by the Child Support Agency (see page 126 for the method of assessment). The court can still deal with periodical payments for the children, if the parents agree. There are to be changes to child support (see page 179).

Availability of state benefits

The court must pay regard to the financial support either party may be eligible for and the effect any court order may have on any state benefit. A lump sum payment can take a person out of benefit. A periodical payment order may stop a person being eligible for housing benefit or other benefit. The provision of the former matrimonial home will not prevent a person being eligible for state benefit, in particular, benefit may be available to cover any outstanding mortgage.

The normal procedure

The procedure set out here is the one which applied in all county courts up until 1997 and in some other courts since then. However, some courts have been running a new procedure called 'the Pilot Scheme'. (See page 74 for the Pilot Scheme.) The Pilot Scheme courts are set out at page 75. From 5th June 2000, it is expected that all courts will be running all cases under a modified pilot scheme (see page 174).

Application

The initial claim for financial relief must be included in the 'prayer' of the divorce petition, or in any answer that is filed. If the financial claim is being made by the petitioner and she wishes to proceed with the application, an application in Form M13 is filed with the court together with the court fee (see page 183). See below for the specimen applications. If the financial claim is made by the respondent where there is no answer, an application in Form M11 is filed together with the court fee. The application is made in the same court and is part of the same proceedings as the divorce. If the case has been transferred to the High Court, the application is issued in the Registry of that court. An affidavit in support of the financial application must be filed with the court with the application. Once the application is issued, the opposing party must be served with the application within four days of issue, together with any affidavit in support. The application should be served on any mortgagee of any property which is being claimed in the proceedings. The affidavit need not be served on the mortgagee, but the mortgagee is entitled to ask the court within 14 days for a copy of the affidavit and has the right to file an affidavit within 14 days of receipt of the affidavit. In practice, the mortgagees rarely take any action in the proceedings since their interest is secured against the property. If a claim is being made against any interest in a pension fund, the trustees must be served with the application and have the right to object to an order within 14 days of receipt.

If one party does not take out a financial application, when he or she is likely to receive an order in their favour, the other party can take out the application on their behalf. It must be remembered that maintenance is only payable until a person remarries, so that if a person has remarried when the court hears the case, they cannot have a maintenance order. If a person remarries before an application for financial relief is filed with the court, he or she is unable to make any claim for maintenance or capital. If the application is made before the marriage and the case is dealt with after the person has remarried, while he or she cannot receive maintenance, he or she can still receive a capital or property adjustment order.

Specimen Financial Claims for Form M11 or M13

The petitioner/respondent applies for:

1 An order that the respondent/petitioner do pay maintenance pending suit.

2 An order that the respondent/petitioner do make periodical payments to the petitioner/respondent.

3 An order that the respondent/petitioner do make periodical payments to or for the benefit of the children of the family namely ____ and ____.

4 An order that the respondent/petitioner do secure to the petitioner/respondent to the satisfaction of the court periodical payments for her life.

5 An order that the respondent/petitioner do pay the petitioner/respondent such lump sum as may be just.

6 An order that the respondent/petitioner do pay to the petitioner/respondent for the benefit of the child of the family such lump sum as may be just.

7 An order that the respondent/petitioner do transfer to the petitioner/respondent all his/her interest in the former matrimonial home/or the property known as ____ registered at HM Land Registry under title number ____. The property is subject to a mortgage of £ ____ in favour of the Building Society/Bank of ____ under roll number ____.

8 An order that there be pension provision and an earmarking order in respect of the respondent's/petitioner's pension with ____ in favour of the petitioner/respondent.

> **9** An avoidance of disposition order (e.g. an order that the
> transfer by the respondent to Mr ____ of the property known
> as ____ and registered at HM Land Registry under title no.
> ____ be set aside) and that such consequential directions as
> may be just may be made.

The application for an avoidance of disposition order is a complex
application and is made where there is evidence that the respondent
has dealt with property with the intention of defeating the
applicant's financial claim. (See page 111.) Where an application is
sought in respect of settled land or the variation of a settlement, a
specific application should be included.

Affidavit evidence

It is the obligation of both parties to give full and frank disclosure
of their financial positions, and the court requires both parties to
advise of any changes in their financial position, up to the time of
the financial hearing. When an application for financial relief is
made, the person applying must file an 'affidavit of means' (a
statement sworn in front of a solicitor or authorised court official)
and served on the other party at the same time as the financial
application. A form of affidavit is available from law stationers and
the courts and is widely used, but it is better in complex cases,
where more detailed information is required, to prepare an
individual one. The affidavit does not have to be in a specific form
but it should include the following.

Information for inclusion in financial affidavit

- Name, address and occupation of the person swearing
  it (the deponent).
- The history of the marriage – the dates of birth of the
  parties, marriage, separation, decree nisi, decree
  absolute (if granted), the names and dates of birth of the
  children of the family, and if they are over the age of 16,
  details of any full-time education they are undertaking.
  If there are children of one party, who are not children
  of both, the same details about those children.

- The capital position, i.e. do they own the former matrimonial home (the property where the family last lived together as a family) – is it in joint names? Does it have a mortgage (or mortgages)? What is its value? A marketing appraisal can be obtained from an estate agent which will give an idea of the value. How much is due to the mortgagee? (The bank or building society will provide a redemption statement which sets out the amount owed to the mortgagee.) What type of mortgage is it: repayment, endowment, interest only? What security is there for the mortgage? Is there a life policy attached to the mortgage? What is it worth? (The life company will provide a current surrender value.) The court needs to know what the proceeds of sale are after the mortgage and sale costs are paid. Sale costs are solicitors' fees and estate agents' commission and are usually between 3.5% and 4% of the sale price.

- Details of other assets or investments, PEPs, TESSAs, ISAs, building society or bank accounts. (Current accounts as well as deposit and savings accounts should be included.)

- Details of any assets of value, say over £500. The court will want the sale value, not the insurance value or purchase cost. A sale value is substantially less than an insurance value.

- Information on the parties' car or cars. What is its sale value? Was it bought on hire purchase? How much is due?

- Details of any pension scheme(s)? This is a complex subject (see page 115).

- The income position. What is the salary of the parties? Is there any other income, such as from investments, interest, dividend income?

- Work details. Does the person work in a partnership or have his or her own business? Is it a limited company or is he or she a sole trader. What is the income from the business? (Drawings/profits/dividends). What is the person's value of the interest in the business. (See page 107). This should be included as a capital asset.

■ If the parties do not work, the reason why not. What qualifications have they and what work have they done in the past? When did they last work? Have they tried to get employment? If not, why not? If they have, steps they have taken to try and get a job should be set out. If the reason is that the person is a full-time mother and housewife, this must be stated. If there is a health reason, this must be stated. If there is medical evidence from a doctor, this can be exhibited to the affidavit. What income he or she expects to receive, if appropriate, should be stated. If some retraining will be necessary, the estimated cost and time it will take should also be stated.

■ Receipt of any state benefit. Child(ren) allowance must be included.

■ If the spouse is giving financial support or paying the mortgage and outgoings (gas, electric, telephone, council tax, house insurances, etc), details of what is being paid.

■ If there are any benefits or perks paid as part of the employment, such as health insurance, company car, free accommodation, pension contributions these should be stated. Are there any bonuses, commission, share option schemes?

■ Any expenses in connection with the employment, such as trade union membership, fares to work, etc.

■ Tax and national insurance that is paid.

■ Any debts, including credit, store, debit and charge cards. Are there bank loans due? Is any other money owed? Are there tax liabilities outstanding for income or capital gains tax?

■ Whether the person expects to inherit any money in the near future (for example in two years).

■ Any interest under any trust – if applicable, the interest, trust deed and how much and when the interest will be paid should all be stated.

■ If the person is claiming a variation to a settlement (a form of trust set up before or after the marriage), details of the trust, the origin of the funds and by whom contribution should be given.

- If the person is seeking an avoidance of disposition, i.e. where a person with the intention of defeating the claim of the other deals with an asset or money so that it is no longer that person's, details of the assets must be disclosed along with the identity of the person to whom it has been transferred.

Example

A husband has 50% of the shares in a successful family company. When he realises his wife is going to bring divorce proceedings, he gives the shares to his brother, so that they are no longer an asset of his, in respect of which the wife can make a claim. The court would treat the shares as if they are a matrimonial asset and transfer them back to the husband.

- The person's 'needs' (outgoings, living costs). A schedule of the current living costs must be prepared. It should be considered whether the living costs will change after the divorce. Will the person move into a smaller property and save money that way? Details of the expected costs should also be included. While some judges pay little regard to the current expenditure of a person, it helps to show the standard of living enjoyed by the family before the breakdown. It is usual for both the husband and wife to be poorer after the divorce, so that it is unlikely that the full amount of the expenditure will be provided. Expenditure should not be inflated: as bank statements and credit card statements are usually disclosed (shown to) the other party and the court, this will be apparent. Remember also that if the expenditure is out of line with the level of income disclosed, this can suggest an undisclosed source of income.
- Intentions as to housing. Does the person wish to stay in the former matrimonial home? Can that be afforded? Can he or she take over the mortgage? (See page 106). If it is agreed that the house be sold, this should be stated and also what type of alternative accommodation is wanted, where and the approximate cost.

Specimen Schedule of Outgoings			
ITEM	**£ – PER MONTH**		**£ – PER MONTH**
Household Outgoings:		**Personal Care:**	
Mortgage/rent		Clothing for self	
Council tax		Hairdressing	
Water rates		Pedicure/manicure	
Electricity		Chiropodist	
Heating/coal/solid fuel			
Gas			
Telephone			
House insurance			
Contents insurance			
Domestic Staff:		**Health:**	
Cleaner		Medical insurance	
Gardener		Prescription charges	
Nanny		Dental charges	
Maintenance of Equipment:		Optician charges	
Service charges for gas		Other	
Service charges for washing machine/dishwasher/other		(Osteopath/physiotherapist/ alternative health care)	
TV/Video:			
Television licence			
Television rental			
Video rental			
Cable/digital			
Property:			
Burglar alarm service charge			
House maintenance and repairs			

Specimen Schedule of Outgoings			
ITEM	**£ – PER MONTH**		**£ – PER MONTH**
Housekeeping: Grocery/food Toiletries Newspaper/books/journals		**Insurances:** Life assurance Pension Health insurance Hire purchase Endowment policies	
Pet Costs: Pet food Pet plan Vet bills		**Other items:** Debts/loans/hire purchase Credit/charge/debit/store cards	
Miscellaneous: Holidays Garden maintenance/plants Entertainment for self Birthdays/seasonal presents Memberships		**Children expenses:** Food (unless included above) Holidays Entertainment Pocket money Children's parties Presents to other children Clubs/after school activities e.g. Ballet/Scouts etc Lessons/extra tuition School fees School uniform Baby-sitting	
TOTAL			

■ Whether the person is co-habiting (living with) or remarried or intending to do either. If a wife is intending to live with or is living with another man, this will have an effect on the amount of maintenance payable. It should be remembered that a person's claim to maintenance ceases on remarriage.

Some courts expect documents to be exhibited (attached to the affidavit) which include the last year's P60, the last three months salary slips, the most recent bank and pension statements. It would be advisable to check with the individual court to find out what is usual.

When the affidavit (or affirmation if the person is to affirm, i.e. to state that the contents is true) is completed, the person making the affidavit should take it to a solicitor (not the solicitor who has prepared it or anyone in his firm) or the court office to swear it. The person will be asked to sign his or her name in the presence of the person taking the oath, and will then be asked to swear on the appropriate religious book (Bible, New or Old Testament, Koran, etc) or to affirm if the appropriate religious book is not available, or the person does not have a religious belief. The usual oath is: 'I swear by Almighty God that this is my name and handwriting and that the contents of this my affidavit is true' or 'I affirm that this is my name and handwriting and that the contents of this my affirmation is true'. If there are exhibits, the additional words 'and these are the exhibits referred to therein' will be added. The fee will be £5.00 plus £2.50 per exhibit.

Once the affidavit is sworn, it cannot be amended in any way. Once a person is served with the financial application and affidavit in support, they have 28 days in which to prepare and file an affidavit, which must set out his or her capital and income position. It should also set out his or her comments on the spouse's affidavit.

Directions

On or after the issue of an application for financial relief a court appointment is set. Some courts will give a date at the time of issuing the application for directions and it is written on the Form M11 or M13. Others may wait until one of the parties asks for an appointment, in which case the Form M11 or M13 will state in respect of the hearing 'on a day to be fixed'. It is then for the person applying to ask the court for a date. When asking for a hearing, the court needs to be given a time estimate (an indication of how long the hearing will take) and what type of hearing: directions, specific matter or final hearing. Some courts automatically list a directions appointment for five minutes and some courts still list all hearings for the same day at 10.30 a.m. although there is no prospect of a hearing taking place until after lunch. It is worth checking with the court office what the practice of the court is before spending a wasted day in court. Some other courts may list the matter for a full hearing, and if the parties want some direction they can apply for a directions hearing. When notice of any hearing is given, the person making the application should notify the other in writing and get an acknowledgement to the letter in case the court does not notify the other party of the hearing and they consequently do not attend the hearing. If the matter is complex and counsel (a barrister – an expert in presenting cases in court) is required, it is important that the barrister is available. Some courts will let you tell them dates that are convenient and others will set a date without reference to you. Some courts will send out with the application their own standard directions, which set out what the parties need to do. If there are no standard directions, directions will be given on the first appointment.

Directions cover the following.

- ■ Affidavit evidence. On the basis that the person applying for the order has filed an affidavit with the application, the first direction is for the other party to file an affidavit, usually within 14 or 28 days although there can be a longer period.

- ■ The person applying is then given leave to file an affidavit in reply, the purpose being to answer any matters raised by the other party. There is no obligation to file such affidavit.

- ■ Disclosure of documents. The parties are entitled to see documents to support any statement in the affidavit. Under the old procedures the court can deal with discovery by ordering that each party prepare a 'list of documents' that are relevant to the application, send it to the other, and then produce those documents to the other party that they want to see. This procedure is cumbersome and results in lots of documents being produced which are not helpful. A procedure has developed whereby disclosure is dealt with by the service of a questionnaire by each party on the other setting out a list of questions on which verification is sought and documents they wish to see, with the other party having to respond within a certain period. This usually means that disclosure is more focused on the documents that are wanted. See page 71 for a specimen questionnaire.

■ Valuation of any assets, particularly the former matrimonial home. The court needs to know what the value is of all the family's assets. Sometimes the valuation can be agreed. Other times there is a disagreement on the value. In this case the court can make various orders. See page 106 for more information.

■ If either party wishes to call an expert witness to give evidence about the value of an asset, the court must give leave (permission) for the witness to give evidence. The court usually wishes to avoid hearing expert evidence because of the substantial costs that are incurred. The court will, if it is satisfied that an expert is needed, give leave but will require that a report by the expert is sent to the other party some time before the hearing and the other party will have the right to produce his own expert's report, which again will have to be disclosed in advance.

■ The court will require the parties to attend court to give evidence and will make an order accordingly for the parties to attend. The court can order the parties to bring with them their wage slips for a period of, for example, three months before the hearing and to bring all savings, deposit and bank statements, again for a stated period that the parties have either in their own name or in joint names.

■ The court can set down the matter immediately (give the hearing date) if the matter is straightforward and the court is sure that the steps that need doing can be done in a reasonable time. A hearing can be 'set down not before the first open day after', which means that the hearing must be set down after the stated date. Alternatively, the court can order that 'the hearing be set down upon certificates of readiness being filed with time estimates', which means that once all the procedural steps have been complied with, a statement is filed, signed by the solicitor, or barrister if one has been instructed, or the individual, if not, saying that directions have been complied with and giving an estimate of how much court time is required for the hearing. A half day is appropriate for a very simple case, but cases can last several days, if not weeks, if there are complex issues and there are a number of experts involved.

■ Some courts order that the parties file up-to-date affidavits immediately before the hearing, to update the financial disclosure. This reflects the fact that due to court delays and the delay in getting to the final hearing, many months may have passed since the original affidavits were filed.

■ Once the directions hearing has taken place, usually no other affidavits can be filed unless the court agrees. If one party's financial position has changed after the filing of the earlier affidavit, he or she can submit a further affidavit setting out the changes and ask the court 'for leave' (permission) to file it.

■ The parties need to provide a copy of the papers for the use by the court at the hearing. The court frequently directs that the 'court bundle' be filed seven days before the hearing. The responsibility is usually on the person applying for the order to prepare the court bundle but it is a responsibility for both parties to co-operate. (See page 90).

■ Costs. The usual order is for 'the costs to be in the ancillary application', which means that whichever party obtains an order for costs at the end of the hearing, will have the costs of the earlier application included.

Specimen Order for Directions

1 The petitioner/respondent do file an affidavit of means and in reply to the petitioner/respondent within 28 days.

2 The petitioner/respondent do have leave to file an affidavit in reply, if so advised, within 28 days.

3 That discovery take place by the exchange of questionnaires within 14 days from the service of the affidavit in 2) above.

4 Both parties do attend the final hearing to give evidence and be cross-examined.

5 The value of the property be agreed if possible, and in default, both parties be at liberty to call one expert witness whose report has been disclosed to the other at least 14 days before the hearing.

In the alternative:

The value of the property be agreed if possible, and in default, of agreement, the parties agree a joint valuer, and in the event that the parties cannot agree a valuer, a valuer be appointed by the President of the Royal Institute of Chartered Surveyors whose valuation shall be binding upon the parties.

6 Not more than 28 days nor less than 14 days before the final hearing the petitioner and respondent do file and serve an affidavit detailing any changes in their financial positions since the date of filing his/her last affidavit.

7 Not less than seven days before the final hearing the petitioner/respondent do file an agreed paginated bundle of documents for the use of the court.

8 The application be listed for hearing on the first open date after two months.

9 Costs in the ancillary relief application.

Disclosure

Disclosure is the stage when documents are provided to verify statements or facts. Reference is made above to discovery by lists of documents. A practice has developed in many courts to deal with disclosure by the service of questionnaires seeking answers to specific information or documents. There is an increasing concern among judges that there are too many documents in any one case which are unnecessary and increase the cost of the hearing. Attempts to see more documents are progressively being restricted. It is increasingly necessary to justify any request for documents. Questions should be focused on issues where further information is required or to elicit the position of the other party on a particular issue, such as their housing need or earning capacity.

Specimen Questionnaire

(Court heading)

QUESTIONNAIRE SERVED BY THE PETITIONER ON THE RESPONDENT PURSUANT TO RULE 2.63 OF THE FAMILY PROCEEDINGS RULES 1991

---

1 Bank and Building Society Accounts

Please produce a schedule of all current, deposit, loan or other bank accounts which the respondent has held in his sole name, jointly with any other person(s) or by his nominee(s), or in which he has or has had any beneficial interest or ultimate benefit, whether in the United Kingdom or anywhere else in the world, in the last *12 months*. In respect of such accounts, please list any other signatory of the account.

2 Please produce a schedule of all building society or other savings and deposit accounts (not covered by paragraph 1 above) which the respondent has held in his sole name, jointly with any other person(s) or by his nominee(s), or in which he has or has had any beneficial interest or ultimate benefit, whether in the United Kingdom or anywhere else in the world, in the last *12 months*. In respect of such accounts, please list any other signatory of the account.

3 In respect of accounts disclosed in 1) and 2) above, please provide copies of statements for the last *6 months* and up to the date of hearing (unless advised otherwise).

4 Of what credit store or charge cards whether or not in his own name has the respondent had the use during the last *three years*. Please produce the statements relating to all such cards for the last *six months* prior to answering this questionnaire (and continuing to the date of trial, unless the petitioner's solicitors give notice to the contrary). Please identify all credit and debit entries appearing in the credit, store account or charge card statements in excess of £100.00.

5 Income

Please provide the respondent's P60 forms for the last two financial years and copies of his pay slips since the commencement of the current tax year and up to the date of the financial hearing.

6 Please provide copies of the respondent's Self-Assessment form for the last two tax years and any assessments raised by the Inland Revenue.

7 Please specify all benefits directly or indirectly enjoyed by the respondent arising out of his employment and state to what extent the same are taxed as such by the Inland Revenue. Please include details of the provision of a motor car and in respect of pension benefits.

8 Holidays – Travel Abroad

Please supply a schedule of all trips abroad made by the respondent during the last two years to the date of answering this questionnaire, stating in respect of each trip:

(a) whether the same was a holiday or in connection with business or both;

(b) by whom the respondent was accompanied;

    (c) the place where the respondent stayed;

    (d) the expenditure incurred by the respondent;

    (e) the source of the funds so expended.

9 Insurance Life Polices

Please produce a schedule of all life insurance policies on the respondent's life and/or of which he is an actual or potential beneficiary and/or in respect of which he pays or has paid the premiums giving in the case of each policy the following particulars:

    (a) the insurance company;

    (b) type of policy;

    (c) sum assured;

    (d) maturity date;

    (e) surrender value, if applicable;

    (f) the presently projected sum inclusive of bonuses payable upon maturity (if applicable).

10 Insofar as this information is not apparent from the respondent's tax returns, a schedule with dates of all dealings in stocks, shares, unit trusts and other publicly quoted investments made by the respondent since the *6th April 200__*. In the case of any such investment which has either cost or yielded, the source and destination of the acquisition cost and proceeds of sale respectively.

11 Please provide full details of any loans made by the respondent or to the respondent including:

    (a) what was the precise date of the loan;

    (b) what was the source of the monies advanced;

    (c) documentary evidence (if possible a cancelled cheque) is requested;

    (d) precisely what representations were made as to the purpose for which the loan is required and the intentions as to repayment;

    (e) what were the terms of repayment and were the same

oral or in writing, and if the latter, produce copies of all relevant documents.

12 Remarriage or Co-habitation Intention

Does the respondent have any, and if so what, intention of re-marriage or cohabitation to or with another woman?

13 General Disclosure Clause

Confirm, if it be the case, that the respondent has neither any source of income nor any capital assets of whatever description or wherever situate, nor any interest in the same, save as disclosed in affidavits that he has sworn in these proceedings and in his answers to this questionnaire, otherwise please give full particulars and produce all relevant documents.

14 Earning Capacity

What is the respondent's case concerning the petitioner's earning capacity.

DATED this _____ day of _____

SIGNED _____

Words in italics can be changed.

A similar procedure is adopted under the Pilot Scheme, see page 84.

The procedure under the Pilot Scheme

This scheme has been in operation since October 1997 and is an attempt by the court to have more control in the management of cases to ensure sufficient information is available at the earliest opportunity and to try to achieve a settlement by court-based mediation. The procedures are running in certain courts and the government has announced that the Pilot Scheme will extend in a modified form to all courts from 5th June 2000. See page 174 for new procedures.

Pilot Scheme Courts

The Principal Registry of the Family Division (the main court for London)

Barnsley	Northampton
Bath	Salford
Blackwood	Southampton
Bolton	Southport
Boston	Stafford
Bow	Staines
Bristol	Stoke-on-Trent
Bury	Taunton
Crewe	Teeside
Guildford	Trowbridge
Harrogate	Tunbridge Wells
Hertford	Willesden
Kingston	Wrexham
Maidstone	

Application

The application is made by filing Form A, prescribed by the rules. The relief sought is the same as in the normal procedure except that if an order in respect of a pension scheme is sought, it must be specified in the application. Once the application is filed, a court-based timetable commences and the court will issue the application and give a date for a first appointment which will take place between 10 and 14 weeks after issue. The application must be served on the other party within 4 days. Under this procedure court hearings are only cancelled or rearranged when there is a good reason.

Timetable – under the Pilot Scheme

■ Week 1

File application for financial relief with the court. Court sets date approximately 12 weeks later for first appointment.

■ Weeks 1 to 7

Preparation of financial disclosure in Form E. Form E exchanged five weeks before first appointment.

■ Week 11

Seven days before first appointment exchange 'statement of issues', questionnaire and 'request for documents'.

■ Week 12

First appointment. Both parties attend. Court gives directions for disclosure of evidence and sets date for 'financial dispute resolution' (FDR) appointment approximately eight weeks later, though this depends on court availability and time needed for disclosure.

■ Week 20

FDR appointment, when the court assists in achieving an agreed settlement. Both parties attend. This appointment can be adjourned. If no settlement achieved, a hearing date is set for final hearing and directions given for the final hearing.

There are some changes to the timetable under the new procedures (see page 175).

Form E

Five weeks before the first appointment, both parties must file a sworn statement in Form E that must be filed with the court and sent to the other party.

Specimen forms can be obtained from legal stationers. It is important to apply for any information which is needed from a third party as soon as possible because it can take some time for the financial institutions to provide the information. In particular, the information should be requested from pension and life assurance companies at the earliest opportunity. If the information has not been provided by the time the Form E is required, it is acceptable to write 'information applied for' and attach a copy of the letter of request. Documents can be attached to the statement to clarify or confirm the position, such as from pension companies.

Information required for Form E

1 Name, address, date of birth and occupation of person making the statement.

2 Date of marriage, separation, decree nisi and decree absolute, if any.

3 Date of any remarriage.

4 State of health of person making the statement and any children.

5 Full names and dates of birth of any children of the family and details of with whom they live.

6 Details of present and future educational arrangements for the children. This should include intentions to go to University.

7 Details of any child support assessments.

8 Details of any other litigation with spouse, for example over specific assets.

9 Details of the deponent's present residence and details of who lives there.

10 Full details of the matrimonial home, including address, Land Registration number, nature of interest, e.g. sole name, joint name, value, name and address of mortgagee, type of mortgage, amount outstanding and current interest in the property.

11 Details as sought in 10 above in respect of any other property.

12 Bank, building society and national savings accounts, including TESSAs including name and address of institution, type of account, account number, name of any other account holder, value at date of statement and interest of the person making the statement.

13 Stocks, shares, PEPs and ISAs including name and type of holding, current value and interest of the person making the statement.

14 Insurance policies including name of company, policy type and number, maturity date, value at maturity and current surrender value, and amount of interest the person making the statement has in these.

15 National savings certificates including original amount invested, current value and interest in these of the person making the statement.

16 National savings bonds and other bonds including bond type and bond holder's number. Current value and interest in these of person making the statement.

17 Debts owed to person making the statement. Include money due from company or partnership.

18 All cash held including the currency it is held in. (Does not include money in a bank account.)

19 All personal belongings worth more than £500 per item. The value is the sale value, not the purchase cost or insurance cost which are frequently three times higher. Includes cars, pictures and jewellery.

20 Any other realisable asset such as unit trusts and investment trusts.

21 Liabilities (excluding mortgages, included elsewhere on form), including credit, store and charge cards, bank loans and hire purchase agreements. If a credit card is repaid in full on a monthly basis, there is no need to include the account. Include any outstanding tax liabilities and give estimated amount if need be.

22 Potential liabilities, such as capital gains tax on any sale of a realisable asset, i.e. sale of shares or investment property.

23 In respect of any business interest, the name and nature of the business, estimated current value of the interest of the person making the statement, estimated capital gains tax on disposal, basis of valuation and net value of the amount of the interest of the person making the statement. It is helpful to seek advice from the company auditor on the valuation and of the estimated tax liability.

24 For each pension scheme the person is a member of, the name, address, plan name and number. The type of scheme, for example final salary, money purchase (see page 118), the earliest date benefit can be taken, the current bid or transfer value, the amount of any lump sum payable on death before retirement (or death in service benefit), the lump sum payable on death after retirement, the lump sum payable on leaving the scheme before retirement age, an estimate of the maximum lump sum payable on retirement, the estimated amount of pension on retirement (it can be useful to attach copies of the letters from the pension trustees giving the alternative information). The pension information is given by the trustees on the basis of 6% and 12% increase. These rates are only estimates and a 9% increase is probably more accurate. The pension trustees should be asked to provide the forecasts on this basis.

A separate page of information should be included for each pension fund.

25 Details of any other asset, including assets which cannot be sold such as share option schemes and interests in trusts including an interest in a discretionary trust.

26 Details of income, including the gross and net figure for the last financial year, i.e. year to the last 5 April, from all employments. The previous year's figure should be available from a P60 form, and the current salary, again gross and net. The net figure is net of tax and national insurance.

27 Details of benefits from employment, including provision of company car or petrol allowance, pension scheme, share option scheme, accommodation. Again, the information is for the previous financial year and current financial year.

28 Details of self-employed or partnership income setting out the net annual profit for the last two accounting periods, the person's share of the profit and estimate of current year income net of tax, and the tax paid, in the last two tax years. The net figure for the profit and loss is the net after expenses but before tax.

29 Investment income including dividends and interest, identifying the asset and stating what the income was in the last and current tax years, and whether it is paid gross or net.

30 Details of state benefit, including state pension and child allowance received in the last 12 months.

31 Details of any other income received in the last 12 months.

32 Future annual needs and those of the children living with the person making the statement. This should include the anticipated expenditure and an estimate of any mortgage needed in the event of rehousing. That figure will have to be an estimate since it will be unclear what capital the person will have in the existing property. See the schedule of expenditure at page 64 above. The children's needs can include private school fees and the extras on the school account, extra curricular activities such as dancing or music lessons, and if the children are not yet at fee-paying school, whether it is the intention of the family that the children be sent to one.

33 Reasonable capital needs and those of the children living with the person making the statement. This includes the housing need and should state whether the person is seeking to keep the former matrimonial home, or if it is to be sold, the estimated amount of a suitable alternative property. It can also include the cost of a major capital expense, such as a new car. The capital needs of the children can include a lump sum to cover future school fees, or a capital sum, if they have special needs.

34 Income and assets of current spouse. This question presumes that the parties have remarried. Usually they have not before the finances are resolved.

35 Standard of living enjoyed during the marriage. This can be difficult to explain, particularly if there is money available but the family have lived modestly. It can help to give a thumb-nail sketch by explaining the type of housing enjoyed by the family, how frequently and the nature of holidays taken, and whether the children are being privately educated.

36 Any particular contributions to the family assets and property made by one or other party to the marriage, setting out the nature of the contribution, the amount, when and by whom. This would include the case if one party brought into the marriage the former matrimonial home or if there was inherited money.

37 Details of any bad behaviour of the other party which the court should take regard of. This relates to the behaviour which it would be inequitable for the court to disregard (see page 54 above).

38 Details of any other circumstance which could significantly affect the extent of financial provision. This includes when one party's earning capacity has been affected by, for example, giving up work to look after children, where there are special needs by reason of a disability, where one party is unable to work due to illness, where there has been a redundancy or where one party expects to inherit in the near future. This does not apply unless the prospect of the inheritance is within the foreseeable future. It would be relevant if the relation is either seriously ill or is very old. It is generally not relevant where the person is in his or her 60's or 70's.

39 The order sought. This should make it clear whether the person either wants or opposes an order for sale of the former matrimonial home. It should set out whether a 'property adjustment order is required' or a 'lump sum order', i.e. a capital sum with which to buy a property. It should say whether a periodical payments order is sought. If it is for a limited number of years, it should be described as a 'term order'. If there is to be no maintenance and all claims against the other are to be dismissed, it should refer to a 'clean break'. If an order in respect of the other's pension fund is sought, this should be stated. These types of orders are described at page 95. It is acceptable to include a statement to the effect that the party cannot give a clear indication of the type of order required until the financial disclosure of the other has been given.

40 If a transfer or settlement of property is sought, information about the asset. This can apply to pension schemes in small family businesses. If a variation is sought to a settlement, the trustees and beneficiaries must be identified and an explanation given defining why the settlement is a 'marriage settlement'.

41 If the person applying believes that the other party has disposed of an asset with the intention of defeating the other's claim, then the asset must be identified as must the person to whom it was transferred.

The statement once completed, must be sworn in front of a solicitor or court official.

First appointment

Seven days before the first appointment both parties must exchange and file with the court the following documents and information:

■ A 'Statement of Apparent Issues' setting out the areas of dispute between the parties in their respective approach to the case.

Specimen Concise Statement of Apparent Issues
(Court heading)

CONCISE STATEMENT OF APPARENT ISSUES
FILED ON BEHALF OF THE PETITIONER WIFE

1 Matrimonial home

The husband puts the value of the matrimonial home at
£ ____. The wife puts it at £ ____.

2 Wife's earning capacity

Wife asserts nil due to ages of children, until youngest child
twelve years old.

Husband asserts wife can work part-time at £ ____ per annum.

3 Husband's income

Wife asserts husband has additional benefits including
company bonus, provision of car, profit related pay.

Husband asserts he received bonus previous year. Not
guaranteed future bonus.

4 Husband's means

Wife asserts husband has Jersey bank account.

Husband asserts money in Jersey held for brother.

5 Value of husband's business

Wife asserts husband has majority interest in company with
substantial turnover, company due to float. Considerable
value.

Husband asserts value of business irrelevant as company not
going to be sold.

6 Wife's co-habitation

Husband asserts wife co-habiting with Joe Bloggs.

Wife denies co-habitation though admits they have gone out
on average twice a week for six months.

7 Housing Need

Wife asserts she should remain in former matrimonial home.

Wife asserts husband can buy 2 bedroom flat for £ ____.

Husband asserts former matrimonial home (FMH) should be sold and property costing £ ____ should be bought instead. Husband asserts needs at least one third of net proceeds of sale as deposit for new three bedroom property costing £ ____.

8 Income needs

Wife asserts needs of £25,000 p.a.(including child).

Husband asserts £13,000 sufficient.

9 Clean break

Wife asserts not appropriate, in view of ages of children, no earning capacity.

Husband asserts clean break appropriate.

Dated _____

Served by (Solicitors for the) petitioner _____

■ A 'questionnaire' setting out the further information sought from the other party. This can include clarification on points in dispute such as the rehousing need of the parties and matters where one party wants an explanation of a statement made by the other in his or her Form E. It can also raise points about financial assets which are not disclosed in Form E. However, a general trawling exercise will not be allowed.

■ A 'schedule of documents' setting out what documents are sought from the other party. The court will usually accept a joint questionnaire and schedule of documents and the information and documents must be more focused than with the questionnaire used under the normal procedure. As the court considers the reasonableness of the questions on the first appointment, the court will only order those questions it considers reasonable to be answered. In particular the court will use its powers to restrict the length of time

for which documents are sought and frequently only
the last six months bank statements and credit card
statements will be permitted.

- ■ Confirmation that all relevant persons have been
  served with the application. This includes the
  mortgagees of the former matrimonial home if a
  property transfer order is sought (see page 58).

- ■ Where an order is sought in respect of the other
  person's pension, confirmation that the pension
  trustees have been served with the application must
  also be given.

- ■ An estimate of the costs (as on the FDR and the final
  hearing).

Under the new procedure, these documents must be served 14 days
before the first appointment and a chronology and a Form G stating
whether that party is ready on the first appointment to proceed to a
FDR appointment. The purpose of the first appointment is for the
court to ensure that the papers are in order and that there is
sufficient information available to both parties and for the court to
resolve the matter by agreement. The extensive disclosure and
investigation available on a fully contested hearing will not be
permitted at this stage.

The court needs to be satisfied that there is agreement over the
valuation of the assets, in particular the former matrimonial home,
and if there is no agreement the court will give a direction for the
valuation of the property. If one or other party has failed to file any of
the necessary papers the court will make an order that party does so,
and may order him to pay the costs of the hearing. The court will
consider the questionnaire and schedule of documents and if the other
party objects to answering the questions or producing the requested
documents, the court will decide whether the party must do so. The
reason for objections might be that the period covered by the request
is too long, that the cost of producing the document will be excessive
in the context of the hearing, that the question has no relevance or that
the question raised is a matter of opinion.

The court will set a timetable for dealing with the directions and
arrange a hearing for the next appointment, state whether further

directions are necessary and, whether there should be a financial dispute resolution (FDR) appointment or final hearing. The court must consider whether the parties should attend a financial dispute resolution appointment, which is a court hearing where the court tries to help the parties reach a settlement by agreement. This is the usual way forward. Only if the court considers that there is no prospect of a settlement being reached will it direct that the matter should proceed directly to a final hearing.

Financial dispute resolution (FDR) appointment

This takes place some weeks after the first hearing when all the directions should have been complied with. If replies to questionnaires are to be completed they should be sent to the other party within the time limit set by the court, together with the supporting documents. The replies, without the documents, should be sent to the court office at the same time. The court does not allow hearings to be adjourned without very good reason.

The purpose of the FDR is for the court to assist the parties to reach agreement, and the court does not have the power to make an order unless the parties consent (agree to it). Both parties and their legal advisers (solicitors and barristers, if instructed) must attend. The hearing is usually listed for an hour, but the court will frequently require the attendance of the parties at court in advance, often an hour or two hours earlier, so that they can negotiate and narrow the issues before the hearing. The judge should have read the Form Es prior to the hearing and replies to the questionnaires and other documents on the court file. A chronology setting out the important facts and a summary of the parties financial positions can assist the court. A chronology is required under the new procedure. The court will not have copies of the bulky documents that are disclosed, so if certain documents are going to be referred to in court, it is useful to have small numbered bundles of documents for the hearing. Copies should be available for the court and the other party. Sometimes a bundle is agreed by both parties. The documents frequently included are details of suitable housing for both parties.

The person applying for the financial order should file details of all offers made, whether 'without prejudice' or not (see page 113), with the court seven days before the FDR. (These will be returned if the

FDR is unsuccessful and the matter proceeds for a full hearing.) A costs schedule will also need to be filed by both parties. The judge should assist the parties by giving indications of the court's approach in respect of certain situations, and if there is a particular dispute, the judge can give indications to help the parties.

> **Example**
>
> Where the wife wishes to remain in the former matrimonial home, but it cannot be afforded, and the husband wants the property sold and a smaller property bought for the wife, the court can give an overview on what it considers reasonable in the circumstances. It has to be noted that there has not been an opportunity for a full enquiry to have taken place so that any settlement relies on the parties trusting that the other has been honest. If there is not that level of trust, it is difficult to reach a satisfactory agreement.

If a consensus is reached, it will be set out in an agreement, drafted by the lawyers and the terms will be explained to the judge who will need to agree that the terms are fair. The court can adjourn the FDR to another date if it is likely that a settlement can be reached in the near future. If the FDR is not successful, the court can give a final hearing date and make directions for the final hearing. These are similar to those set out in the normal procedure (see page 70). The judge who hears an unsuccessful FDR is debarred from hearing the final hearing. If agreement is reached after the FDR, the court can be asked to make an order by lodging a 'minute of order' (the agreed terms) with the court (see below). The court may also require a statement of financial information (Form M1) to be filed with the court (see page 88).

Consent orders

At any point, even before an application for financial relief is filed with the court the parties can agree the terms of settlement and ask the court to make an order. The terms are set out in a 'minute of order'.

It is important even when matters are agreed between the parties, that the court is asked to make a court order. It is only once there is a court order that there is any certainty. Where there are no proceedings for financial relief, the court will require that if the respondent to the divorce proceedings is also the respondent to the financial application, that he or she file a notice of application for financial relief in Form M11 with the words at the top of the form 'dismissal purposes only'. This is needed because if the court is to dismiss financial applications, the rules require that there is such an application on the court file. No separate fee should be payable on the application. Some courts may require a Form M13 to be filed by the petitioner, again with the same words at the top, if one has not been filed already. Some courts take the view that if there is a 'prayer' (request) for financial relief in the divorce petition, that will be sufficient (see clean break orders and specimen clean break order at page 97).

Documents to be lodged for consent order

■ Minute of order (which should be filed in duplicate with the court).

■ Application in Form M11 or M13, as appropriate, marked for 'dismissal purposes only'.

■ Court fee (see page 183).

■ Statement of financial information, (Form M1).

The Form M1 is a global statement of the capital and income of the parties and is in a prescribed form. Each party can complete their own form, or the information can be included in a joint form.

Information required for Form M1

1 Ages of the parties, children of the family and length of marriage.

2 The net capital of each parties. This is after liabilities, so, for example, the value of the matrimonial home is included less the mortgage.

3 The net income of the parties, i.e. after tax and insurance.

4 The value of the parties' pension funds showing the current transfer value.

5 Confirmation that the application has been served on any mortgagees and pension fund trustees, if there is an order which effects either the mortgagee or a pension earmarking order and they have not objected to the application within 14 days of service of the application.

6 Any other circumstances. Sometimes an order on the face of it will not seem sensible and it can help to explain the circumstances which make it a reasonable order.

7 Whether each party has an intention to or has remarried or is cohabiting.

When the papers are lodged, the court will consider the terms and if the judge considers them fair, will make an order as requested. Where one or both do not have lawyers advising, the court may require a short hearing to make sure that any unrepresented party understands the order and has entered into it freely. The court is entitled to raise questions about the terms and can make amendments to the order, although these are frequently only as to the phraseology used and not the effect of the order. The court will frequently return the order to the party who is making the application with the judge's comments on the back-page. The minute of order should be amended or the enquiries dealt with, either by a joint letter from the parties' solicitors, or sometimes by having a short appointment before the judge to clarify the difficulty raised.

Once the order is agreed, copies are sent by the court to both parties. A consent order has the effect that the parties cannot usually appeal against it if they subsequently change their minds.

The final hearing

Preparation for the hearing

After the directions hearing, whether the case has come via the Pilot Scheme or through the usual route, the next stage will be the final hearing.

The first step is to comply with the directions. If there are directions permitting experts to give evidence, there will be a direction that the expert's reports be exchanged. It can help if the opposing experts can meet to discuss the evidence and narrow the areas of dispute. The directions will provide for obtaining the hearing date, either by filing certificates of readiness or by giving a date. If counsel are instructed, the court should be notified of the availability dates of counsel and any witnesses, including the husband and wife.

A bundle of papers should now be prepared for the hearing. Depending on what directions are given, it is usual for the person applying for the financial order, to prepare the documents. From May 2000 a court bundle must be prepared by the applicant and filed two clear days before the hearing. It can assist if both parties agree the bundle. The bundle should be clearly paginated and indexed.

Example court bundle

Section 1 The financial papers including application and orders.

Section 2 Statements and affidavits.

Section 3 Expert reports and other reports.

Section 4 Questionnaires and replies. (Sometimes the questionnaires can be omitted if the questions are included in the replies.)

Section 5 Applicant's financial disclosure.

Section 6 Respondent's financial disclosure.

In addition, at the start of the bundle there should be a summary of the background to the case, statement of issues, summary of orders sought, chronology and where appropriate skeleton arguments.

It is not necessary to include all the documents which have been disclosed and it is preferable to restrict the documents to those that are going to be referred to during the hearing, otherwise there can be a penalty in costs. Unless they are relevant, years' worth of bank and credit card statements should not be included. Statements for the last three months will give an example of the expenditure pattern. Documents showing the most recent valuation of assets such as PEPs should be included.

If there has been a delay in the time between the original disclosure and the hearing date, it may be necessary to update the disclosure and to obtain up-to-date bank statements, etc. It is helpful to update any expenditure to show the needs of the parties particularly the wife, if she is claiming maintenance. It also helps if the person seeking a new property visits several suitable properties before the hearing and produces realistic property details to show the cost of alternative housing. For example, if the former matrimonial home is a three bedroom property worth £200,000, a range of two bedroom properties costing £125,000 to £150,000 should be produced. Details of properties for the opposite party can also be produced in the same way. If a mortgage will be necessary, enquiries should be made about the current mortgage being transferred into the sole name of the other, or about raising a new mortgage based on the likely financial position of the person applying. Alternatively, some mortgage costings should be made available for the court.

Any court bundle should be paginated (numbered at the bottom of each page), with a detailed index. The draft index should be given to the other party to agree. Sometimes it can be agreed without difficulty though an objection may be taken to a particular document being included. Those documents which are not agreed can be included in a separate bundle. Some courts like the court bundle filed with the court before the hearing and the directions will set out what is required. Sufficient copies of the court bundle should be available for the court. This will include the judge, a witness bundle and the advocates. It is usual to provide a copy of the index to the other party, and if they require a complete copy of the court bundle, this is also to be provided. It is important to comply with the directions order. If a barrister is to act, a conference should be arranged for the barrister and the client a week or so before the hearing so that any steps the barrister wants to take can be executed before the hearing. Arrangements should be made for the expert witnesses to be available to come to court.

It is becoming more usual for the applicant to prepare a summary of the assets of both parties and a chronology of the marriage for the use of the judge. Lawyers are now preparing written submissions (statements setting out their arguments) regarding their cases. It is important that any such document is fair – it should not use emotive language or show only one side of the case. A copy of any such chronology or written submissions should be given to the other party before the hearing and, unless there is any objection, handed to the judge to read before the case starts. A statement of costs will again be required.

Example chronology

1 Petitioner wife name. Date of birth, age.
2 Respondent husband name. Date of birth , age.
3 Date parties met.
4 Date co-habitation commenced.
5 Date of marriage.
6 Children's full-names and dates of birth.
7 Date of separation.
8 Date of divorce petition.
9 Date of decree nisi and decree absolute (if appropriate).
10 Date of financial application and relief sought.
11 Dates of financial affidavits/financial statements.
12 In addition, include dates of property purchases and sales if relevant, dates of career/job changes, date of starting own business.
13 Other significant events likely to have a bearing on the outcome of the hearing.

If there is a legal point and reference is to be made to case law (a previous case), a list of authorities (case names and reference numbers) should be filed with the court the previous day so that the court can have a copy of the case(s) referred to available.

Alternatively, particularly in smaller courts, it helps to have copies of the case reports available for the judge and the other party.

If there are children involved, the court expects to be given an indication of what amount would be payable if an assessment for child support was carried out.

What happens at the hearing

At the hearing the person who has applied for the financial application will start proceedings, unless, for example, the husband has applied for the wife's financial claim, in which case, as it is the wife who is seeking financial relief, she, or her lawyers, should start.

The person making the application (whether a lawyer or lay person) must explain the background to the application and at this stage the chronology and summary of assets can be handed in, if not done so earlier. The applicant should explain to the court what type of order (periodical payments, clean break, etc) is required and explain briefly and fairly the background to the marriage and what he or she is asking for.

It used to be the practice for the affidavits to be read aloud to the judge, but that practice has virtually stopped as the judge will usually have read the affidavits before the hearing. Nevertheless, an opportunity must be given for the judge to read the affidavits and statements. Reference can be made to the court bundle and the judge can be referred to any particular document. It is becoming less common for the 'opening' to be long-winded. The applicant will then usually be called to give evidence first and will be 'sworn in'. He or she will stand up and will take the oath using the appropriate religious book. The applicant will then be asked his or her full name and address by his or her lawyer (solicitor or barrister, if one is instructed) and will be asked questions about the case. The lawyer will have discussed the evidence before the hearing with the applicant and will know what answers are expected.

The point of the questions is to expand on any aspect of the case which is unclear on the court papers. The etiquette is that the applicant's case must be set out at this point. If aspects of the applicant's case are not put to the applicant at this stage, the lawyer may not raise the point at a later point, i.e. in 're-examination'. If there are areas in respect of the respondent's case which are not agreed, if the applicant is able to give evidence about the point, the question must be put to the applicant in 'examination in chief'.

When the applicant has finished giving evidence, the opposing party will ask questions (cross-examination). These questions may be quite testing as the opponent is trying to show the court a different set of facts from the one shown to the court. Again, where there is a dispute by the respondent over the applicant's case, there is a duty for the applicant to be asked about the disputed matters and to have the chance of responding. If the matter is not put to the applicant, the respondent may be unable to give evidence on this point later. It is important for the applicant not to lose his or her temper or to answer questions in a flippant manner.

Once the cross-examination is completed, the applicant's own lawyer can ask some further questions (re-examination), provided those questions relate to matters raised in cross-examination and are not new issues. The judge can ask questions as the matter proceeds and frequently asks for clarification at this point. The applicant will then call any other witness he or she is calling, including any expert evidence (although quite often a time is set aside when both parties' experts are present together to give evidence and hear the views of the other).

The procedure for evidence to be given is the same for all witnesses. When the applicant has finished presenting his or her case, the opposing party presents his or her case and the procedure is repeated. When the evidence is completed, the respondent can address the court and 'sum up' the evidence. The applicant's lawyers will finish by restating their aims and summing up the evidence. It is at this stage that case law is referred to and any cases which are relevant are referred to. A judge can indicate that he wishes to be 'addressed' about certain aspects of the case and the evidence, and he or she is entitled to raise matters at this point.

Where a person is representing themselves without lawyers, the procedure is the same, but a judge will usually try to assist the person in giving evidence and should be lenient if the matter is not presented as well as it would be by a lawyer. Sometimes an objection is taken to a question being asked by the opponent. This is either because the question is asked as a 'leading question', i.e. phrased in such a way that the answer is given in the question, or because it concerns a matter which is not relevant to the issue before the court. The rules of evidence and how to ask questions which are not 'leading questions' are an art of their own and cannot be dealt with in detail here. If a case is so complex that the rules of evidence are necessary, it would be advisable to use lawyers.

The judge is likely to adjourn the case before he or she delivers judgement, either over lunch, or sometimes a further hearing will be necessary. The judge will usually give a judgement in which he or she sums up all the evidence he or she has heard, indicate whether he or she believed any of the witnesses, and whose evidence he or she prefers if there is a dispute of fact. He or she can give judgement in court with the parties present, or can deliver a written judgement. Once the judge has decided the case, the question of who should pay the costs is dealt with (see page 158). Once judgement is delivered, a written order has to be produced and this is often prepared by the applicant's lawyer, and agreed with the other party and then filed with the court. A formal order will be drawn up by the court and sent to both parties. Fourteen days are given in which to appeal.

Types of order

Periodical payments

A periodical payments order is one where payments are made monthly (or weekly) and the order will state:

Periodical Payments Order

The respondent (or petitioner) do pay to the petitioner (or respondent) the sum of £ _____ per annum, payable monthly in advance during the parties joint lives, until the petitioner (or respondent) do marry or further order.

It can be useful to have the maintenance paid by standing order to the recipient's bank account and an undertaking can be included as follows.

Standing Order Provision

Upon the petitioner/respondent undertaking to the court to make the periodical payments order hereinafter ordered by bank standing order to the respondent/petitioner's bank account number ____ with bank ____.

In some cases, where there is ongoing maintenance, and the parties' respective financial positions are such that the paying party will only have inflation proofed salary increments, an order providing for the automatic increase of the spousal maintenance can reduce difficulties in the future. A suitable clause would be as follows.

Inflation Proofing Clause

The periodical payments ordered hereafter shall, in the event that there shall be any increase in the Retail Prices Index over the twelve-month period ending with (March) in any year from and including 2000, be increased by the percentage of such increase with effect from (June) in each such year.

Maintenance is only payable to a spouse until the recipient has remarried and while both the payer and recipient are still alive. The court has the power to vary an order in the future, the basis of such an application being that the financial circumstances have changed. This can be either by the payer applying if for example he or she has been made redundant, or the recipient if over time the amount ordered has been eroded by inflation.

If the recipient co-habits (lives with another person) for a period of six months, very often the maintenance is stopped. Strictly, the court will take this into account on an application to vary, but the means of the co-habitee will be taken into account and if, for example, the co-habitee is without means, the order for periodical payments may be reduced to take account of the economy of two people living together but may not be stopped. Again, if the co-habitation stops, the recipient can apply for an upward variation of maintenance, but the court can be unwilling to recommence a maintenance order.

Periodical payments are usually ordered where there is a non-working wife who is looking after children, as the court can reconsider the position as necessary, and in particular when the children no longer require a full-time mother. The court does have the power on a variation application to stop maintenance altogether and has been given power to stop maintenance on the basis of a further lump sum payment.

Where the circumstances are such that at the time of the determination the wife, for example, is not entitled to an order for periodical payments but there are circumstances where she may become entitled to a substantive order, an order for a nominal amount (e.g. £1.00 per annum) may be made, which can be varied at a later date if appropriate. It may be useful where both parties are working and approaching retirement age and the wife does not have a future pension and need to claim on the husband later. The clause is:

Specimen Nominal Order

The respondent do make to the petitioner during joint lives until such time as she shall remarry or further order periodical payments at the rate of £1.00 per annum.

Clean break

A clean break order is one where periodical payments are paid and both parties claims for financial relief against the other are dismissed. This means that neither can apply at a later date for capital or income or against the estate of the other, should the spouse predecease.

If the parties agree that neither should have any claim against the other unless there is a court order dismissing the financial claims of the other, an application can be made at a future date, either during the life time of the other or against the estate of the other. Under the

Inheritance (Provision for Family and Dependants) Act 1975 where one party dies, the other can make an application for financial help out of the estate of the deceased. The only way for this claim to be stopped is by an order of the court dismissing the claim. See the example below which is a standard 'clean break order', i.e. neither party has a claim against the other during their lives or against their estates. A claim can also be made against property under the Married Woman's Property Act 1882 and the order should include reference to this act to avoid subsequent claims.

Example Clean Break Consent Financial Order.

(Court heading)

MINUTES OF AGREEMENT AND CONSENT ORDER

---

1 UPON the petitioner and the respondent acknowledging that the provision referred to hereafter is accepted in full and final settlement of all claims the petitioner and respondent may have against each other for both capital and income or other property adjustment and in respect of pension entitlement including claims arising under the Matrimonial Causes Act 1973 (as amended), the Married Women's Property Act 1882 (as amended) or any claim which may arise under the Inheritance (Provision for Family and Dependants) Act 1975.

2 AND UPON the petitioner and respondent agreeing that the contents of the former matrimonial home have been divided (alternatively: have been divided in accordance with the attached schedule).

3 AND UPON the petitioner and respondent acknowledging that they have no further claims the one against the other in respect of chattels and otherwise under section 17 of the Married Women's Property Act 1882 (as amended) **AND** it is further agreed that each party is to retain ownership of the assets under his or her control.

BY CONSENT that upon decree nisi being made absolute it is ordered:

1 The petitioner's and respondent's claims for maintenance pending suit, periodical payments, secured periodical payments, lump sum and property adjustment orders to stand dismissed and the petitioner and respondent shall not be entitled to make any further application under section 23(1)(a) or (b) of the Matrimonial Causes Act 1973 and pursuant to section 15 of the Inheritance (Provision for Family and Dependants) Act 1975, the court considering it just to do so, neither the petitioner nor the respondent shall be entitled on the death of the other to apply for an order under section 2 of that Act.

2 There be no order for costs insofar as this application and the negotiations ancillary thereto are concerned

DATED the _____ day of _____ 200 __.

SIGNED_____   SIGNED_____
(Solicitor for) Petitioner   (Solicitor for) Respondent

The court has the obligation to consider making a clean break order on all applications. Where there is a short marriage with no children, or where both parties are in good employment and self - sufficient, a clean break is appropriate.

Sometimes it is appropriate for there to be some financial provision such as the transfer of property or payment of a lump sum. In calculating the amount payable the amount required for the parties needs should be taken into account, to include the housing requirement and the maintenance need based on the realistic living cost. Where the family have sufficient resources, and where there is an imbalance in the incomes of the parties, it may be possible to provide a sufficiently large lump sum to provide for the income needs of the recipient for their estimated life expectancy. The calculation known as a Duxbury calculation was named after a case of that name. In *At A Glance*, published annually by the Family Law Bar Association the Duxbury calculations are included as a rough guide. The court no longer adheres strictly to the Duxbury calculation but it is used as a guideline. Where there are a number of special factors an individual calculation can be carried out either by an accountant or a specialist lawyer.

Advantages and Disadvantages of a Clean Break Settlement

Advantages

Financial obligations to the other ceases.

Both become financially independent.

No future variation of the order.

No claim against the estate of the other.

No loss of income for recipient on remarriage.

Recipient has lump sum to invest as he/she wishes.

No risk to payer if the recipient loses his/her employment or ability to work in the future.

Disadvantages

Raising the capital sum, if money not available.

Prospect of paying too high a lump sum if recipient remarries after order.

Inability for recipient to benefit from payer's subsequent financial success.

Financial responsibility for the recipient.

There is a concern that where a clean break order has been made on the basis that no spousal or child maintenance will be payable, it is not possible to give up a claim under the Child Support Agency and if state benefit is claimed, then an application may have to be made for child support and this may be payable. The following wording is appropriate where the order provides for a transfer of an asset, such as the former matrimonial home:

Specimen Order where there is a Capital Payment and there is to be no Child Support Assessment

Narrative

That the parties have agreed that the financial provision herein satisfies the petitioner and the children of the family namely and ____ claim on the respondent for financial provision and the petitioner agrees not to apply for an assessment under the Child Support Act 1991.

Order

The property known as ____ do stand charged in favour of the respondent (or the petitioner do pay to the respondent a lump sum of) an amount equal to the total of any sums payable by the respondent under any assessment under the Child Support Act 1991 in respect of the said children.

Term order

A term order is one that states that maintenance is for a term of years and then dismissed. If it is in simple form the recipient is able to apply for the period of periodical payments to be extended beyond the original term, provided the application is made before the original period has expired. This gives a degree of protection for a husband as the court will consider whether periodical payments should continue after the original date and the court can take into account the circumstances in the intervening period. For example, if a recipient has become disabled through illness and is unable to work, the court may extend the maintenance period.

Specimen 'Simple Form' Term Order, which can be Extended

From the date hereof during their joint lives, until the petitioner's remarriage, or until the (date) whichever shall be the sooner, the respondent do pay the petitioner the sum of £____ per annum payable monthly in advance whereupon the petitioner's claims for periodical payments and secured periodical payments shall stand dismissed and the petitioner shall not be entitled to make any further application in relation to the marriage for an order under section 23(1)(a), (b) or (c) of the Matrimonial Causes Act 1973 in relation to the marriage.

It is possible to stop the court extending the initial period. This is called a 'section 28(1)(a)' directive and states:

Specimen Term Order which cannot be Extended

From the date hereof during their joint lives, until the petitioner's remarriage or further order or until the (date) whichever shall be the sooner, the respondent do pay to the petitioner the sum of £____ per annum payable monthly in advance, and the petitioner's claims for periodical payments and secured provision shall stand dismissed and the petitioner shall not be entitled to make any further application in relation to the marriage for an order under section 23(1)(a), (b) or (c) of the Matrimonial Causes Act 1973 in relation to the marriage **AND IT IS DIRECTED** pursuant to the Matrimonial Causes Act 1973, section 28 (1)(a) that the petitioner shall not be entitled to apply under section 31 of that act for an extension to the term of the above order.

A term order is used when it is reasonable to expect a cut off for maintenance in the future, and it is clear when that date will be. For example, as when children attend full-time secondary school it is reasonable to expect the mother to work and for the husband's maintenance for the former wife to cease.

The court is reluctant to make such an order if there is not some certainty that the recipient will become independent financially, i.e. whether a mother will be able to get a job and be independent when children are aged 11. It can also be appropriate where there are no children and the wife needs maintenance for a limited period to retrain to get a job and become independent financially.

Child maintenance

The court historically dealt with periodical payments orders for the children of the family (and for children not of both parties to the marriage but treated as if children of the family). The Child Support Act 1991 was intended to deal with all cases of child relief except for certain situations such as where one or other parent lives abroad, or the child is over the age of 18.

Because of the complexities of the child support calculation, the court is frequently invited to make an order by consent for child maintenance in a sum similar to that which would be payable under a child support assessment. Where there is child maintenance, there is frequently spousal maintenance, so that the figure of child maintenance and spousal maintenance would be calculated to cover the total need of the household. See page 125 for explanation of child support.

Child Maintenance Order

An order for periodical payments for children is defined in the Matrimonial Causes Act 1973 as being:

'Until the child attains the age of 17, or completes their full-time education if later, or further order.'

This is because the obligation to pay child maintenance continues until the child is 17 or completes full-time education, if later, which includes university, college, school and training for a trade profession or vocation.

This type of order is appropriate where there are younger children and it is unknown how far they will progress with education.

Where there is a teenage child and it is intended that the child should go to further (tertiary) education, the order can refer specifically to the age of 18 or until such time as the child completes his or her secondary or indeed tertiary education. If a state grant may be available for tertiary education, it can be helpful for the obligation to pay maintenance to continue until the child finishes his or her schooling, since a grant is usually assessed on the basis of the child's income and that of the residential parent.

If there is an order for child maintenance, as it is still possible for there to be a child support assessment, it is necessary to include a clause to allow for a claw back. See the capital claw back provision (page 101).

Where the wife receives maintenance, and the figure for maintenance for the wife and children has been worked out globally, there can be a claw back provision if there is subsequently a child support assessment.

Specimen Claw Back Out of Maintenance where Subsequent Child Support Assessment

In the event of the respondent being required to make payments under an assessment following an application under the Child Support Act 1991, the respondent shall be entitled to a £ for £ reduction to the periodical payments order in favour of the petitioner by the amount that the child support assessment exceeds the amount provided herein for child maintenance.

Where the children attend fee-paying schools, an order for the school fees can be included as follows:

Specimen School Fees Order

The petitioner/respondent do pay or cause to be paid to the child _____ from the _____ day of _____ until he/she shall attain the age of 17 years or until he/she completes his/her full-time education (whichever is the later) or further order periodical payments for herself/himself :

1 Of an amount equivalent to the school fees and the agreed extras on the school account at the school the said child attends for each financial year by way of three payments before the commencement of each school term.

2 The sum of £ _____ per annum, payable monthly in advance in respect of general maintenance of the said child.

3 It is further ordered that part of the order that reflects the school fees and said extras shall be paid to the Headmaster/ Bursar/School Secretary as agent for the said child and the receipt of that payee shall be a sufficient discharge.

This clause allows the paying party to pay the school fees direct to the school in case there is a concern that the mother would not pay the school fees. Prior to 1989 there were tax advantages to divorced parents paying maintenance to children and school fees as the benefit of the child's personal allowance and lower tax rates were available. Save for orders made prior to 1989, no tax relief is now available so that the benefit of a school fees order is reduced. The tax relief available on the pre-1989 orders has been abolished since 2000. An 'undertaking' from the paying party to pay school fees could alternatively be included in the order.

If there is no spousal maintenance and the parents have not remarried, then the child maintenance can be paid to the former spouse on behalf of the child to obtain the now limited tax relief on spousal maintenance. It is limited to 10% of the equivalent of the married man's allowance and ceases in 2000. The clause is:

Specimen Maintenance Order for Child in Favour of Parent

The respondent do make or cause to be made to the petitioner for the benefit of each of the children.

An order for child maintenance can be inflation proofed (see page 96), but as a child's needs change faster than the rate of inflation, it may be better not to include such a clause.

See also under child support (page 125).

Orders in respect of the former matrimonial home

Where there is an order for the transfer of the former matrimonial home from one spouse to the other or an order for sale of the property, the order should state 'Liberty to apply', which gives the parties the power to ask the court for further help if there are difficulties over the sale.

If there is an order for sale, it helps to avoid confusion to state in the order who is to sell the property, the timetable for the sale, who is to decide on the agents and who chooses the solicitors.

It is easier if the party living in the property should instruct the solicitor so that any purchase can be tied in with the sale. It is likely the co-operation of both parties will be required to deal with the conveyancing procedure and, if the property is in joint names, to sign the property documents.

Sometimes it is appropriate that one party should remain in the property until the youngest child reaches a certain stage in his or her education, usually, when he or she completes secondary school. If the other party, usually the husband, is to receive some capital when the property is sold, the property can be transferred into the sole name of the wife and the husband can take a second charge over the property to ensure he is paid his money on the sale. A properly drafted charge should give the husband the power to force a sale when the time comes if the wife refuses. In this situation, consideration must be given to the mortgage and, if the husband is to be released from the mortgage obligation, the wife will need to apply for the mortgage to be transferred into her sole name.

Where there is a transfer of property between a husband and wife, or former husband and wife, if a certificate is included in the transfer that it is a matrimonial disposition, stamp duty should be avoided. Land registry fees will be payable, but should be at a reduced rate.

While the transfer or sale of a property would normally attract capital gains tax, where the former matrimonial home is transferred under a court order, there is a special exemption and capital gains tax will not arise provided one of the parties has lived in the property as the principal home (unless the person transferring it has made an election for capital gains tax purposes in respect of another property). Capital gains tax will arise on a transfer of property if it is not the former matrimonial home.

Special financial considerations

Where a family's assets are particularly complex or there is a dispute over the value of the asset, special directions can be applied for, but the court is not prepared to allow costs to be incurred unnecessarily.

Valuing assets

Where there is a dispute as to the value of a particular asset, usually the former matrimonial home, both parties can bring evidence of its value if the court allows expert evidence to be called. There is little point in spending a lot of money valuing an asset of little realisable value – such a jewellery (see specimen clause page 70). Usually the experts' reports must be exchanged before the hearing and some courts now require the experts to meet before the hearing to try and agree the valuation.

Value of a company/partnership

In looking at company and partnership interests it must be appreciated that if the business is the source of the family income that it is unlikely to be sold. In addition to the income derived from the business (either paid as a salary under PAYE, or as director's fees, dividends or share of profits) there may be a capital value for the shares or other interest in the business. If the business owns freehold premises, these have a value. A trading company may have stock. There may be cars or machinery owned by the business. In addition, there may be money owed on a partnership loan account or director's loan account.

The starting point is to look at the company's accounts for a period of at least three years, and these should be available in the case of a limited company from Company's House. The question to ask is whether the gross income has increased or reduced over the period and whether there have been any other changes in the figures which are out of line with its trading position. If pension contributions have increased since the breakdown of the marriage, that can suggest that the pension holder is protecting his future interests.

If the wages bill increased out of line with the gross income, this may suggest that monies are being drawn as a salary rather than as profits.

The accounts should show whether there are leasehold or freehold premises and surveyors can be asked to value them. The company may have a recent valuation and the 'notes to the accounts' may explain any valuation. If there is an intention to sell the business in the foreseeable future or possibly to float it on the Stock Exchange, the value becomes more significant. It is appropriate to raise questions about the company in any questionnaire, such as the following:

Specimen Questions Regarding a Small Family Owned Limited Company Business/Partnership

1 The respondent has disclosed his interest in —— Limited. Please confirm whether the respondent has been a proprietor and/or partner and/or in business during the last three years and, if so, supply full particulars thereof together with full corroborative documentary evidence in respect of any business other than —— Limited.

2 Please provide details of all directorships held by the respondent within the last three years.

3 As to the company —— Limited and any other company disclosed in the reply to question 1 above, please provide

(a) Copies of the accounts of the company (if necessary in draft) for the last three years.

(b) If the accounts of the company for the year ended 200__ are not yet available, even in draft, when is it expected that their preparation will be completed? A letter from the company's accountants explaining the position is requested.

(c) Copies of any existing management accounts in respect of the last six months.

(d) The company ____ Limited owns freehold premises at ____. Have there been any, and if so what, professional valuations of the land and buildings in question during the last three years? If so, please produce copies of the same. In any event what is the respondent's estimate of the open market value of the said assets.

(e) Identify all company cars owned by ____ Limited, identifying the make and year of manufacture of each motor vehicle and identify when it was purchased and who is the main or principal user.

(f) Please confirm that, upon reasonable notice, the accountants instructed on behalf of the petitioner/respondent in connection with these proceedings will be granted the facility to inspect the company's books and other documentary records.

(g) Please provide a copy of the memorandum and articles of Association of the company.

(h) Have any and, if so, what plans have been canvassed between the respondent/petitioner and/or his/her fellow directors of the company and/or the company's professional advisers as to the possibility of the company being publicly floated, whether on the unlisted securities market or otherwise. If so, copies of all documents relating thereto in the custody, possession or power of the respondent are requested, including but not limited to all Minutes and Memoranda of any Board or other meetings in which the possibility of such flotation has been discussed. Please confirm in any event the company's minute book will be made available for inspection on request.

(i) Has the company (or the respondent/petitioner, personally) received any offers, approaches or overtures for its acquisition by any person or by another corporate entity as a going concern? If so, full particulars are requested together with all documents relating thereto in the custody, possession or power of the respondent/petitioner, including but not limited to all Minutes and Memoranda of any Board or other meetings in which the possibility of such a flotation has been discussed. Please confirm in any event the company's Minute Book will be made available for inspection on request.

4 Please provide a copy of the company's private ledger or other documentary record of all movements which have taken place on the respondent/petitioner's loan or current account between _____ and the date of answering this questionnaire and continuing thereafter until the date of the hearing unless the petitioner/respondent's solicitors give notice to the contrary.

5 Please explain the source and determination of all credit and debit entries respectively which appear in the said ledger or record insofar as the same are not apparent therefrom.

Income

6 Please provide a schedule of all director's remuneration, including salary, fees and bonuses received by the respondent/petitioner during the last three years.

7 Does the respondent/petitioner have any expectation of an increase in his/her remuneration during the foreseeable future? If so, please give full particulars.

8 Please provide copies of the three forms P11D most recently submitted to Inland Revenue together with the accompanying claims under section 198 of the Income and Corporation Taxes Act 1988.

9 Please specify all fringe benefits directly or indirectly enjoyed by the respondent/petitioner arising out of his/her employment by the company and state to what extent the same are taxed as such by the Inland Revenue. Please include details of the provision of a motor car and in respect of pension benefits.

10 Please provide a copy of the respondent/petitioner's service contract and copies of all correspondence passing between the respondent/petitioner and his/her employers which contain reference to the terms upon which he/she is employed.

11 Please provide details of any dividends paid to the respondent/petitioner by _____ Limited over the last three years.

If there is some apparent value in the business the court may agree that a forensic accountant be instructed to look at the business and value it. A specific direction will be required from the court including provision for the exchange of reports and the attendance of the experts.

It should be considered whether it is possible for any benefit to be obtained from the business without it showing in the accounts. This can include undisclosed cash, i.e. cash which is not recorded and shown in the accounts. If there is income being withdrawn from the company without being shown in the accounts, one indication can be where the family income is far lower than the level of the family's expenditure.

> ### Example
>
> If the business accounts and the husband's disclosed income show a share of profits of £20,000 gross per annum, but the family is spending £40,000 a year, it is possible that there is undisclosed income. A forensic accountant can check whether the accounting processes are such that there could be undisclosed income and can check the gross income against the disclosed net income and see if it accords with the trade normal.

In valuing shares or an interest in a partnership, account must be taken of the size of the interest. If it is over 50% it will have a higher value than one less than 50%, and any shareholders agreement and company documents or partnership agreement will need to be checked to see if there are pre-emption clauses (i.e. requiring the shares to be offered to another person before being sold and whether the method of valuing the shares is set out in the agreement).

Hiding assets

Where one party has taken steps to hide or dissipate his or her assets with the intention of defeating or reducing the financial claim of the other, the transaction can be set aside (reversed) by the court. Sometimes the circumstances warrant an application being made to the court to prevent assets being hidden before the final determination of the financial application. This requires very quick action.

If there is evidence that the party is about to or has taken such steps, an injunction (an order from the court ordering a person to do something, or not to do something, sometimes called a section 37 order) can be sought as an immediate remedy.

If it is suspected that the other person is going to take such steps, an undertaking from the person confirming that they will not do so can be given in correspondence, but it does not have the same effect as an undertaking given to the court, breach of which amounts to a contempt of court for which a person can be imprisoned. It may be necessary to take steps to stop a party disposing or dealing with assets and the court has a general power to make such an order, sometimes called a 'Mareva injunction' (a freezing order). Such an order can apply to assets which are not in England and Wales. Again, in exceptional circumstances, the court may make an order to allow a person to enter and search and remove relevant papers. This is called an 'Anton Piller order'.

Where a person is likely to leave the country and by so doing will prejudice the other party's case, the court may make an order *ne exeat regno* (that the person does not leave the country until a sum of money has been deposited for safe keeping with the court). This is a very rare application and is given before the financial application is decided by the court. It is given frequently with a Mareva injunction. Alternatively an order can be obtained that a person must deposit their person's passport(s) with the applicant's solicitor for safe-keeping.

Where assets have been moved, an application needs to be made specifying the action taken and seeking its reversal. Specific reference needs to be included in the financial relief application (see page 58).

The effect of bankruptcy

Where one party, for example, the husband, has been made bankrupt, the capital assets will pass either directly to the trustee in bankruptcy (if they are in the husband's sole name) or the equitable interest in the asset will pass to the trustee (if the asset is in the joint name of husband and wife). This has the effect of putting the asset outside the ambit of the family court and any dispute over property ownership and equitable rights will fall to be resolved in the bankruptcy court where the principles of contribution apply, i.e. each party gets back what they have contributed unless an equitable interest has arisen through the rules of equity. The bankruptcy court has no power to adjust the interest in the family asset to take account of the wife's non-financial contribution.

If, which can happen sometimes as a result of too harsh a settlement, or through spite, the husband goes bankrupt after the financial order is made, the bankruptcy court can set aside any transfer of property made within three years of the bankruptcy, on the basis that it is considered to have been made with the intention of defeating a claim by the creditors. A liability under a financial order does not fall within the bankruptcy, so even if the Trustee in bankruptcy pays a high dividend out of the estate, the wife does not benefit. Her liability will remain and she will have to seek payment once the husband is out of bankruptcy which usually lasts three years.

If the husband proceeds with an individual voluntary arrangement rather than a bankruptcy, which has a lot of advantages, then if the wife has an existing financial order, she is entitled to be a party to the IVA proceedings. If she does not have a financial order at the time of the IVA, she is not a creditor at the time of the IVA and is not affected by it, she can proceed with her financial claim, but this can lead to a direct conflict between her and the creditors.

Negotiations

There is now an obligation on both parties to try to resolve matters by agreement without the court's intervention.

The court will look at the way the matter has been conducted by both parties and following changes to the 'Civil Procedure Rules' in 1999, will take this into account when dealing with the question of costs. It is important, therefore, to be aware that the court may see any correspondence not marked 'without prejudice' and accordingly letters should not use emotive language or express the personal view of the writer.

Obligation defined

The obligation is on both parties to negotiate and to put forward their respective cases at the earliest opportunity. The intention is to protect a person who makes a reasonable offer of settlement from the costs of the litigation continuing if the other party refuses the offer. It is not acceptable, therefore, for a wife when receiving a reasonable offer, to not respond either by acceptance or a counter-offer.

There are changes due in June 2000 which are relevant (see Chapter 6, page 177).

Negotiations can be conducted as follows.

■ In 'open correspondence', i.e. correspondence which the court is entitled to see.

■ 'On a without prejudice basis' in which case the letters must be marked 'without prejudice' and are not shown to the court (save in certain applications such as the Financial Dispute Resolution (FDR) Appointment, see page 86).

■ As 'Calderbank' correspondence, see below.

It is useful to explain in any letter of settlement the reasoning behind the offer and to include all the proposed terms of the settlement. Once an agreement is made in correspondence, even without prejudice correspondence, the agreement can become binding on both parties and the court can be asked to make an order on the basis of the agreement. The court will not make an order if there has been undue pressure from one party, if full details of the other person's financial position have not been given, and where an agreement is entered into without both parties, in particular the weaker party, having independent legal advice.

'Calderbank' correspondence

'Calderbank' is the name of a case in which it was accepted that correspondence could be written making a proposal in family cases which would have the same effect as making a payment into court in an ordinary civil dispute. It may now be called a 'section 36 offer'.

In matrimonial cases, the main asset is usually the matrimonial home and until it is sold there is no money available with which to make the settlement.

If correspondence is written in this way and marked either 'Calderbank offer', 'section 36 offer' or 'without prejudice save as to costs', then the court is unable to see the letters before the judge decides the case. Once judgement is delivered, the party who made the offer, if the amount offered is more than the amount awarded, can ask the court to order the other party to pay the costs after the date of the letter (or after a reasonable period of time to consider the offer). For there to be an effective Calderbank letter, full financial disclosure must have been given and there is no obligation to negotiate prior to full disclosure being given. At the financial hearing it is useful to have available a numbered bundle of Calderbank correspondence to produce to the court once judgement has been given. It is important that the judge should not be aware of the correspondence before he has decided the case.

Wording for a Calderbank Letter

This letter is written under the principles laid down in *Calderbank v Calderbank* and we reserve the right to refer the court to it on the question of costs.

See new costs rules page 177.

Pensions

Under the old law, pensions were relevant to a financial settlement but the court was not able to make any order that affected the pension fund. This is because while the pension is a fund in which the person has an interest, it is not held by them but on their behalf.

In 1996, under the Pension Act 1995, 'earmarking' became available. This is where the benefits of the fund are held for the benefit of the spouse, but still remain the entitlement of the pension holder and are treated as such for tax purposes. The important point to remember in respect of pension and death benefit is that on the death of the party paying periodical payments, the order for periodical payments to the survivor ceases. In many pensions, on divorce, the widow's pension will be lost.

There is a need to provide for the non-pension holder after the death of the paying party. This is not always possible and if it is a problem some years in the future, in view of what may happen in the intervening period, it may be reasonable to rely on the protection given to a former spouse under the Inheritance (Protection for Family and Dependants) Act 1975 whereby she can apply for financial provision (both income and capital, provided claims have not been barred in any court order) out of the estate of the paying party, and the court will consider what is reasonable in the light of the position at the time.

Promises have been made by parliament that 'pension sharing' will be introduced. This is now due in 2001.

The benefits of 'sharing' will be that the pension fund is separated at the time of the financial settlement and held separately for the husband and wife, so that the non-pension holder will be able to draw her pension independently from the pension holder.

It is likely that the new legislation will apply to divorces commenced after a date as yet to be announced. It may be desirable where the pension funds are significant to delay the petition until the new legislation is in force. That said, people have been waiting for years already and the new law may never arrive because of the complexity in drafting the legislation.

It must be appreciated that the quantification of pension rights is a highly specialised area and the guidance of the parties financial advisers should be sought. Because pensions are usually drawn in the future, the figures available are only estimates and will depend on market forces for the individual funds. If the pension holder dies, the pension will stop and the non-pension holder is then exposed. Consider taking out some life cover on the pension holder, or an assignment of an existing life policy. Another aspect to consider is the benefits that have yet to accrue to the fund.

> **Example**
>
> The husband who is 60 years of age is a member of a final year's scheme. There are five years to retirement age, so the pension holder will be making a further five years worth of contributions to the scheme. Under English and Welsh law the court can take account of the benefits at the time of the divorce and those that which will accrue afterwards. This, therefore, includes contributions made after the divorce.

There is a trend towards dividing the fund by reference to the actual years of marriage, although this will require a complex actuarial calculation at the time of drawing the pension.

The powers that are available to the court

Adjournment

The court can adjourn the financial hearing or part so that the pensions can be dealt with at a time when the pension holder actually retires and adjournments up to five years have been given. This is only appropriate when retirement within a few years is likely.

Allocation of non-pension assets

Where there are substantial non-pension assets, it may be possible to meet the non-pension holder's needs by giving him or her a greater share of the liquid assets. This is called 'offsetting' and we have seen above (page 99) this can be done by a capitalisation of maintenance under a Duxbury calculation.

Delay Decree Absolute

As the widow's pension is usually lost on divorce, if there are insufficient other assets to buy out the non-pension holder's claim, the court can consider not making the decree absolute, absolute. A two year or five year petition can be blocked if it would cause grave financial hardship to allow the decree absolute. That could include the loss of a widow's pension.

Earmarking

This is where the benefits are 'marked' for the non-pension holder and the pension trustees can be ordered to pay the entitlement to the non-pension holder. The pension holder still has control over the fund and it is only when the pension holder retires and draws any benefit, that the non-pension holder can receive any benefit. The fund is treated for tax purposes as that of the pension holder. The court can direct that the pension trustees should pay money direct to the non-pension holder.

It applies where the divorce petition was issued after 1 July 1996 and the financial application has been filed after the 1 August 1996. Earmarked orders for periodical payments are by their nature maintenance orders and accordingly cease on the remarriage of the recipient. An earmarked lump sum order will still be payable, notwithstanding remarriage of the non-pension holder.

The Court's Powers Under 'Earmarking'

The court may order the trustees to pay:

■ all or part of the pension to the non-pension holder by way of maintenance;

■ all or part of the commuted lump sum to the non-pension holder;

■ death in service benefits, or a part, to the non-pension holder.

Loss of widow's pension

On divorce, whereas the non-pension holder would normally be entitled to a widow's benefit on the death of the pension holder, that benefit is usually lost unless the pension policy pays benefits to a former wife within the definition of dependants. Even if there is a dependant's pension, that can be lost on the remarriage of the pension holder as the widow's benefit would go to the new wife.

It is possible to calculate the loss of the widow's pension by taking the age difference between the husband and wife, the years to retirement and the estimated amount of the widow's pension. The calculation is set out in *At A Glance.*

This method of compensating the non-pension holder is appropriate where there are many years until the pension holder will retire and where the fund values are relatively small. It is also relevant where there is a clean break settlement as the lost pension can be quantified in capital terms.

Different types of pension

Final salary occupational pension schemes

These schemes apply for civil servants, teachers and doctors and nurses in the National Health Service. The benefit is based on the number of years service (i.e. working for and being a member of the scheme) against final salary.

> ### Example
>
> A man with 30 years worth of pensionable service has a final salary of £60,000 per annum and the pension is in 60ths, so that he has 30/60ths X £60,000 = £30,000. If the wife is entitled to 50 %, she would get 50% X £30,000 = £15,000.

Money purchase

This type of scheme is frequently used by the self-employed or given as part of a company scheme. A fund is accumulated in an investment, and when the pension holder retires, the money is invested in a pension fund. At this point a lump sum can be taken and different types of pensions purchased such as inflation proof, guaranteed income for limited period, pension to last life, etc. These policies are sometimes one-off premiums and sometimes require a regular contribution. It is important to ensure that, if a value of the fund is taken on the basis of future contributions, there is an obligation to pay those obligations.

Specimen Undertaking to Continue Making Contributions to Personal Pension/Retirement Annuity Pension

UPON the petitioner/respondent undertaking to the court to continue contributions of £ ____ per month/year to the policy/contract number ____ until the petitioner's/respondent's retirement/drawing benefits on (date) save in the event of the petitioner/respondent being obliged to accept early retirement on the grounds of redundancy, invalidity or ill-health or becoming ineligible to continue to pay any contributions, the petitioner/respondent to inform the respondent/petitioner within ____ days of either of the aforesaid events.

Small company executive pension scheme

With some small company schemes where the only member of the pension scheme is the main shareholder of the company, it may be possible to make the wife a member in her own right if she has worked for the company at some time, and then proportion part of the husband's entitlement to the wife by setting up a sub-trust for the benefit of the wife. It will be important if this device is to be used that no other member of the pension scheme's entitlement will be effected. The pension trustees must be approached for their view on whether this is viable.

Benefits defined

Pension benefits may come in one of the following ways:

■ Lump sum death benefit before retirement paid to the pension holder's estate on his death while he is still employed; after he has left the employment but before drawing the benefits; and sometimes there is a guaranteed period for payment of the pension for that period.

Frequently the lump sum is a multiple of the contributions made. Schemes frequently for tax reasons have the benefit payable as a discretionary benefit and the payment is made by the trustees in accordance with a letter of wishes. The court can require the pension holder to nominate the non-pension holder in respect of all or part of the lump sum.

Specimen Undertaking for Lump-Sum Payment from Occupational Pension Scheme

AND UPON the petitioner/respondent undertaking to the court irrevocably to nominate within ____ days from the date of this order that the respondent/petitioner/children of the family shall for so long as the periodical payments order contained in paragraph ____ below shall subsist (or as appropriate) receive £____ (__%) of the lump sum payable in the event of his or her death in service under the ____ pension scheme and to provide upon request by the respondent/petitioner written evidence of receipt by the trustees of the ____ scheme of such nomination.

■ Widow's benefit payable to a widow whether on death-in-service or on death-after-retirement. Usually the widow's benefit is the same whether the pension holder dies before or after retirement, and is usually calculated as a percentage of the pension holder's pension, frequently 50%. This benefit is often lost on divorce by reason of the remarriage of either the pension holder or the non-pension holder. It may be possible to take out insurance on the pension holder's life (in which case the pension holder's co-operation may be needed with any life company) or to take an assignment of an existing policy to provide protection for the wife and if there are minor children, the children. The husband will frequently be willing to assign an existing policy to a former wife so long as she has not remarried, with provision for it then to go to the children.

Specimen Order

The trustees or managers of the pension schemes do pay or cause to be paid to the petitioner on behalf of the respondent the widow's benefit provided the periodical payments order in favour of the petitioner shall still subsist at the date of death of the respondent.

■ Lump sum on retirement. Under tax legislation a percentage, currently 25% of any pension fund, can be commuted (converted into a lump sum) with an immediate cash payment being made on retirement and thereafter a reduced pension. The lump sum can be a very useful benefit coming at the time the pension holder retires and while it represents income, as the pension will be reduced, if the spouse does not have a periodical payments claim, then it can be treated as a capital asset and included in the assets available for division. Frequently the non-pension holder receives between a third and half of the lump sum. As there is no obligation on a pension holder to withdraw the lump sum, it is important to impose on the pension holder an obligation to draw (commute) the maximum lump sum as follows:

Specimen Undertaking and Order

Undertaking

AND UPON the respondent undertaking to the court to draw the maximum tax free lump sum available on retirement in respect of his pension with ____ pension fund _____

Order

AND provided the petitioner shall not have remarried at the date of the respondent's retirement under the terms of his pensions aforesaid the trustees or managers of the respondent's said pensions do pay to the petitioner on behalf of the respondent a lump sum equivalent to (50%) of the maximum lump sum payable to the respondent upon his retirement under the terms of the said pensions.

Any such payments shall be treated as payments by the respondent as the party with pension rights or towards his liability under the order.

■ Pension payable to the policyholder. The court can order that either a fixed amount or a percentage be paid to the non-policy holder as periodical payments. If the wife is to receive part of the pension under an earmarking order, she must be entitled to periodical payments at the time of the retirement, so that a clean break dismissal of her maintenance is not appropriate. She will also lose the benefit on her remarriage. A direction can be given to the pension trustee/manager for the share of the pension to be paid direct to the non-pension holder. It must be remembered that the pension is treated as the pension-holder's for tax purposes and will be paid net of tax by the pension provider. The non-pension holder receives the payment tax free as it represents periodical payments.

Specimen Order

The pension trustees/managers of the pension fund do cause to be paid to the petitioner on behalf of the respondent __% of the net pension payable thereunder payable monthly in advance out of the retirement pension due to the respondent herein, provided the petitioner shall be in receipt of periodical payments at the date of the respondent's retirement, during their joint lives, until the petitioner shall remarry or further order. Payment made by the pension trustees/managers be treated as payments made by the respondent to the petitioner in accordance with his obligations contained herein.

Valuation of the fund

The value of the fund is taken as the cash equivalent transfer value, which the pension trustees or the fund's actuaries can calculate. This is the value of the accrued rights under the scheme at today's date and is similar to the amount which would be paid were the pension holder to leave the scheme and transfer the money to a new scheme.

The value does not include the death-in-service benefits, any discretionary benefits and future benefits.

Procedure

An application for an earmarking order is a type of financial relief and applies where divorce petitions are issued after 1 July 1996 and the financial application is issued after 1 August 1996. A specific claim must be included in the application for financial relief (whether Form M11, M13 or Form A) and should specify the key terms of order sought in respect of the pension. The application must be served on the pension trustees or managers and they have 14 days to respond.

Because of the complexity of the individual pension rules, it can assist to get the pension trustees/managers to approve the draft order before it is made. Once an order is made, the beneficiary should ensure that the trustees are advised of his or her interest and are kept aware of his or her address, his or her banking details and any change to his or her marital status. Because it is possible for the pension holder to avoid or reduce the potential entitlement, the following should be ensured.

■ An obligation to continue to pay contributions to the scheme.

■ An obligation to stop pension holder moving the funds or reducing fund value.

Specimen Undertaking

The respondent will not draw any benefits from the ____ pension fund in such a form as to frustrate the provisions for periodical payments and lump sum orders as provided hereafter without the written consent in writing of the petitioner, such consent not to be unreasonably withheld.

The respondent will not transfer his pension rights in the ____ pension fund to any other pension policy or scheme without the written consent of the petitioner, such consent not to be unreasonably withheld.

■ An obligation that the pension holder will retire and draw his benefits by a certain age. If the respondent does not retire or decides against drawing the pension, the petitioner would not receive the benefit.

Specimen Undertaking

The respondent undertakes to take all his benefits under his pension in the pension fund no later than his 65th birthday.

■ An obligation that the pension holder takes sufficient benefit to meet the order.

Specimen Undertaking

The respondent undertaking to take all benefits under his pension with ____ pension fund in such a form that there will be sufficient net annuity and capital sum available on commutation to meet the requirements set out at paragraphs hereafter.

■ An obligation to keep the non-pension holder advised of his intention to retire.

Specimen Undertaking

The respondent undertakes to give the petitioner 28 days notice of his intention to retire or draw benefits under his pension with pension fund.

■ An obligation on the pension holder to authorise the pension trustees or managers to give information to the non-pension holder.

Specimen Undertaking

The respondent undertakes irrevocably to authorise the pension trustees/managers of the _____ pension fund to release to the petitioner such information as he/she may from time to time require relating to the said policy.

Child provision

Before the Child Support Act 1991 came into effect, the court had to deal with periodical payments for the children. Since then, child support can either be dealt with under the Act or by the court, with agreement, provided the parent with care (the parent with whom the child lives) is not in receipt of certain state benefits. The court based procedure is set out above.

Child support

Child support applies where both parents and the child live in the United Kingdom. The procedure was introduced with the intention of using a formula for determining the level of child maintenance to be paid by the absent parent (the parent with whom the child does not live). There is to be a new scheme in 2001 (see page 179).

Where the parent with care (the parent with whom the child lives) is on state benefit she is obliged to apply for child support, unless she can satisfy the Secretary of State that there is a reasonable risk that she or the children will suffer harm or undue distress. If there is not, the parent can be penalised by a reduction of 40% of the income support allowance for up to three years. It is not a sufficient excuse that the parent does not wish the absent parent to be aware of her whereabouts.

Child support applies to children who are:

- under the age of 16;
- under the age of 19 and in full-time schooling;
- under the age of 18 and registered on a youth training scheme.

Procedure

If one parents decides to apply for child support, a Maintenance Application Form (available from the Child Support Agency) is completed. The Child Support Agency send a Maintenance Enquiry Form to the, other parent to complete within 14 days. Detailed financial information is required by the agency including details of his or her gross and net income, living expenses, details of all their children, details of whether he or she lives with another person and whether there are any other children in that family unit.

The calculation is carried out by the Agency and takes into account the living requirement of the child and the parents. If the absent parent is on certain state benefits, his income is treated as nil and he will not have to pay child support.

An interim assessment can be made if the absent parent has refused to co-operate. If the absent parent denies parentage of the child the court can order that there are blood samples given to determine parentage (see page 156). The assessment is based on calculating the following.

- The maintenance requirement, which is based on the child allowances (for the relevant ages of the children), plus

   family premium, plus

   lone parent premium, plus

   adult personal allowance, less

   child benefit.

- The exempt income, which is based on
  personal allowance, plus
  family premium, plus
  lone parent premium, plus
  housing costs.
- The assessable income is the net income (which is the
  gross income less tax, national insurance and 50% or
  pension contribution) less exempt income. 50% of the
  assessable income is paid towards the maintenance
  requirement. Where both parents work, the income of
  both parents is taken into account and the exempt
  income for both parents is calculated to determine the
  assessable income. Once the maintenance requirement
  is met, the absent parent contributes 25% of his
  assessable income up to a ceiling set by the regulations.

If the assessable income exceeds the ceiling, a 'top up order' may
be made by the family court on an application for the court to
determine what money should be paid by way of child maintenance
in addition to the child support.

Example

John earns £28,000 per annum gross, £22,000 per annum net,
no pension and has two children aged 8 and 10 by Sarah.
Sarah earns £6,000 per annum gross, £5,200 per annum net.

(i) The maintenance requirement:	**John**	**Sarah**
child allowance	–	£53.20
plus		
family premium	–	£15.90
plus		
adult personal allowance	£52.20	£52.20
less		
child benefit	–	£27.55
TOTAL MAINTENANCE REQUIREMENT	£52.20	£93.75

(ii) Exempt income:		
personal allowance	£50.20	£50.20
plus		
child allowance **plus**	–	£53.20
family premium **plus**	–	£15.90
housing costs	£150.00	£80.00
TOTAL EXEMPT INCOME	£200.20	£199.30
(iii) Assessable income:		
net income,	£384.00	£100
less		The net income is
exempt income	£202.20	less then the exempt
		income so is ignored.
TOTAL ASSESSABLE INCOME	£181.80	
50%	———	
TOTAL CHILD SUPPORT	£90.90	

The assessment takes into account the time the child spends with the absent parent. If it is over 104 days per year, there is a pro-rata reduction of the child support payable. If an assessment is wrong, an appeal is available.

When the Act came into force the original assessments were significantly higher than the level of periodical payments the court had been ordering previously. There was also no way of deviating from the assessment calculation if there were particular circumstances. Because of the inflexibility in the system, a variation to the rules was introduced to allow for a 'departure direction'. This is a ruling by the Secretary of State that due to certain circumstances, as defined by the Act, the normal calculation should not be carried out, but a new figure should be used for the assessment. The departure directions apply in the following circumstances.

- Special expenses in travel to work, travel to maintain contact with child, costs connected with long-term illness, debts incurred before the marriage breakdown, which were joint debts of the parents, or for the benefit of any child.
- Where, prior to April 1993, there was a property transfer order to the parent with care and there was, or should have been, a reduction to the level of maintenance, as a result.
- Where the assets do not produce income.
- Where there is a diversion of income.
- The person's lifestyle is inconsistent with disclosed income.
- Unreasonably high housing cost, partner contributes to living cost or travel cost too high or should be disregarded.

Application is made in writing by either party.

Child maintenance

The court can make a secured order for a child so that if it is felt likely that a father will not honour his maintenance obligation and assets are available, the assets are secured (charged), and in the event that the maintenance is not paid, the assets are used to cover the liability. This can be helpful where, for example, there is a need to meet school fees and the family have capital assets, but the income, or the willingness to pay maintenance by the father is uncertain.

School fees

See page 104.

Lump sum orders

The court has the power to make a lump sum award to the child of a family on divorce under the normal application for financial relief, although it is more usual for the lump sum payments to be made to the wife rather than the children. There is also power to apply for financial provision under the Children Act.

Capital provision for children

While not made in the divorce, a stand alone application can be made for capital and indeed housing provision for minor children. Where there is a divorce, such claims are made by the mother on her own account in the divorce rather than on behalf of the children.

Appeals

Where a financial order is made by a district judge, an appeal can be made to a circuit judge at the same court, provided the appeal papers are lodged within 14 days of the order. (An appeal can be filed after the 14 days if the court consents.) The appeal is by way of a rehearing with the facts and determination of the first judge being the basis of the hearing of the appeal. New evidence can be heard if there have been particularly relevant events. The appeal judge has to decide whether the judge decided the case properly and even if the judge considers the judgement to have been wrong, whether it is so wrong that he or she should change the decision.

If a financial hearing is heard by a High Court judge, an appeal lies to the Court of Appeal.

Enforcement of a financial order

If the order is not complied with there are steps available to enforce the order. It is relevant whether the order was given in the High Court or the county court as different procedures apply to certain remedies.

If the arrears are in respect of periodical payments, arrears of more than a year old can only be enforced if the court agrees (gives leave). An application to enforce the arrears is usually made on the affidavit setting out the terms of the order, the amount of the arrears, the address of the debtor and if the application is not made in the court where the original order was made, a copy of the order. The application is usually made in the court nearest the debtor's home.

If it is a payment of a lump sum, interest is usually payable on the amount which gives some protection.

Enforcement procedures include the following.

- Application for an oral examination of the debtor. This is to ascertain the debtor's financial position and then choose which method of enforcement is the most appropriate. The debtor must provide full details of his finances. (This course is frequently not required as this information should have been available at the financial hearing.)

- Warrant of execution

  This is a procedure whereby the court agrees to instruct the court bailiff to enforce the order by taking possession (walking possession) and then sale of the goods of the debtor. Certain items cannot be sold such as a bed and tools needed for the debtor's trade. It is a straightforward procedure and the costs of taking the action should be recovered from the debtor as well.

- Judgement summons

  An application is made to the High Court or county court in the area in which the debtor is living. The order sought is that the debtor should go to prison on the basis of his wilful refusal to pay the money. The court examines the debtor's means and is entitled to make a new order with regard to the payment of the debt and can waive the arrears if it appears that the debtor cannot pay the debt. The court can send a debtor to prison if he or she fails to attend court or if the court considers he or she has the means to pay but has refused to. The court will usually order a suspended order so that the debtor is given extra time to pay the debt.

- Attachment of earnings order

  This is an order directed to the debtor's employer and ordering the employer to deduct an amount from the debtor's wages and pay the money to the court.

- Garnishee orders

  An order directed to the debtor's bank or creditor ordering that the monies held or owed to the debtor be paid to the applicant. The affidavit in support must identify in addition to the usual information where the funds or property are and give the reason why the applicant believes the money are due to the debtor. The hearing is in two stages. First hearing for an order to the creditor to explain why the money should not be paid to the applicant, and the second hearing for the creditor to object to the payment, if appropriate. The first order must be served on the creditor.

■ Charging order

An order charging the debtor's interest in a fund or property and amounts to an equitable charge. An order once obtained can be enforced by a sale of the property.

■ Transfer of property

If the court orders that the former matrimonial home is to be transferred by one party (for example, the husband) to the other and the husband refuses to execute (sign) the property transfer document, the district judge can sign the transfer document on his behalf.

■ Liberty to apply

This is required in an order where there is an order for sale of the former matrimonial home (or indeed other property). This gives the parties the right to come back to the court and seek further directions (orders) from the court to help with the selling of the property. Problems can arise if, for example, the wife is in occupation and will not co-operate over allowing access to estate agents or prospective purchasers. The court can make further orders to require her co-operation.

4 | THE CHILDREN

This part covers the arrangements for the children on divorce and the legal process. It includes different patterns for contact with the non-resident parent and deals with arrangements where the resident parent lives abroad.

Terms defined

Until the Children Act 1989 came into force, the court had to make an order in respect of the children and the terms used then were 'custody', 'care and control' and 'access'.

The court's approach to children on divorce has changed radically and the aim now is to obtain the parents agreement over the children and to reduce the hostility which occurs when there are contested proceedings. The terms now used are parental responsibility residence and contact.

The 'children's interests are paramount', and that means the court will decide each case on what is best for the children. Although in some divorces the issue is that the father does not have as much contact as he would like with the children, in the greater number of cases the difficulty is that the father does not want as much contact or as regular contact as the mother may want or considers to be beneficial for the children.

Disputes over the children must be handled sensitively and it is better to compromise the issue than to have a fully contested hearing in court.

Two years after divorce (for whatever reason) less than 50% of fathers have regular contact with their children. As there are more and more divorces and remarriages and sequential relationships, more and more children are being brought up in complex family situations, with step-brothers and -sisters and step-parents, and the difficulty over maintaining contact with both parents becomes harder and harder the more children and relationships there are.

It should be remembered that while at the time of the marriage breakdown emotions run high and the children can become a major issue, the fact is that a parent's relationship with a child will (or should) last much longer than the child's childhood. If contact is maintained at some level in the early stages of divorce, it can be built upon, and by the time a child is a teenager, the child will be able to express his or her own preferences regarding the arrangements. Contact with a child as a teenager or young adult is much harder to re-establish if it has been broken off following a divorce. Children, as they mature, will also be able to judge the behaviour of the parents and decide with whom to maintain a relationship in adulthood. It is important to remember that when, in later life, a child marries or graduates or there is some other happy event, both parents will wish to be present.

Children must be protected from the conflict between the parents and must not be exposed to criticism by one parent against the other. All matters regarding children are treated with the strictest confidentiality by the court.

What is a 'child of the family'?

The court on divorce is concerned with the following.

■ Children of both husband and wife, born before or after the marriage.

■ Children of either parent and who have been treated by both parties as a child of the family.

Any such child must be under the age of 16 or over the age of 16 but under the age of 18 and full-time in school, college or training for a trade, profession or vocation. To be treated as a 'child of the family' means the child has been treated by both parents as if it were their child and this extends to matters of upbringing, discipline, where the child lives and who provides for the child financially. This therefore includes children of both parents and step children.

The current terms defined

Parental responsibility

All parents of children born when the parents were married, or married after the child's birth, have parental responsibility which is the entitlement to take the important decisions about a child.

These include:

- the religious upbringing of the child;
- the medical treatment for the child;
- the educational upbringing;
- all other important matters.

On divorce, the court now rarely makes an order for parental responsibility unless there is a special issue. Because parental responsibility is conferred by being the parent of the child, it is now normal for both parents to share it as it is considered better for the child to have the involvement of both parents.

In certain circumstances, parental responsibility can be taken away from the parents by the courts, or from one of them and given to Social Services. This happens only where there are serious concerns for the children, such as that a child is being abused.

What can a parent with parental responsibility do?

- Each parent is entitled to act independently of the other (although it is preferable for there to be consultation and agreement between parents).
- A parent can change the name of the child, but if there is another person with parental responsibility, then the consent of that other person must be obtained in writing, but see under residence orders (page 137).

Example

Mother has remarried and wants her child from her previous marriage to have the same surname. Father objects. The court will decide whether the name can be changed, though is reluctant to agree the change. If the father does not object, the name can be changed without a court order. See the position if there is a residence order, below.

A parent may stop the other parent, or anyone else, taking the child out of the country without the written consent of every person with parental responsibility.

However, if there is a residence order however, in favour of, for example, the mother, neither parent can take a child abroad even for a holiday (save for the mother for a period of one month a year) unless the other parent's consent is given in writing.

A parent with parental responsibility can apply to the court for leave to take the child out of the country, if consent is not forthcoming (see page 143 for procedure).

Residence

Residence is where the children make their primary home.

The court does not normally make a specific order for residence on divorce.

While twenty years ago children nearly always lived with their mother, it is now more common than it was for the children to live with their father.

If a father applies for residence, it is still usual for there to be some failing on the part of the mother in her ability to care for the children for him to be successful. This is usually due to alcohol or drug abuse or neglect. Foreign courts recognise the concept of residence, and it can be helpful where the parents come from different countries for there to be a residence order.

If there is a residence order, say in favour of the mother, she can take the children abroad for up to one month in a calendar year without the consent of the other parent or the leave of the court.

Where there is a residence order in existence, no one may change the surname of the child without the leave of the court. There can be an order for 'joint residence' where the parents live separately but the child spends time living with both parents, such as one week with one and the next with the other. This is still rarely given, as in such cases the parents tend to agree on matters and there is no need for a court order, but it can only work where there is a high degree of respect and co-operation between the parents.

Contact

Contact is the term used to describe the arrangements for the non-resident parent to see the children.

Parents should have contact with the children when they are available to spend time with them. The pattern of contact will need to be flexible and reviewed periodically as the children get older and have their own activities to take into account – an arrangement that works well with pre-school children, may not work well when they are older. The amount of travelling must also be considered both for the party having contact and also for the children. It will not help the relationship if the children spend two hours travelling each way in a weekend visit to their father. In those circumstances the father should have longer periods less frequently and should get the contact visits over bank holidays, school holidays and half-terms.

For babies and pre-school children, the father should have frequent contact, particularly a baby or young child, who will not remember the father if there are long delays between visits.

When there are great conflicts between the parents, it can help if family and friends are used to help with the collection and delivery arrangements, either by accompanying the parent who is collecting the children, or by arranging for the children to be 'dropped off' at the friend's house so that the parents do not meet.

The arrangements will depend on the father's ability and willingness to care for the needs of young children, and whether the children will suffer if they are away from their mother for a period.

If a father has not seen the children for a while arrangements should be built up over time. Initially it can help for the contact to take place in familiar surroundings, possibly even the former matrimonial home or a relation's home. Contact should develop so that the father can have the children in his own home and the relationship can develop naturally.

Where children are teenagers, they will be able to decide where they wish to live and the court will listen to their wishes. Arrangements previously made sometimes change as children move to secondary school and become more independent. They may then decide to live with the other parent.

Considerable conflict can arise where the father insists on having contact in the former matrimonial home; it is an infringement of the wife's independence and not appropriate.

Where there are likely to be difficulties over the arrangements, it is better to be more specific in an order and detail all the arrangements and who is to do what and when. This should include who fetches and delivers the children. If the mother is going to be uncooperative, it may be better for the father to do the travelling. It is usual for the parent with whom the children are to be to collect them so that a father collects at the beginning of a contact visit and the mother at the end.

Difficulties sometimes arise when one parent forms a new relationship. It is unreasonable to expect the new partner not to come into contact with the children. If it is the mother who has a new partner, the father can feel his place is being usurped. The mother should ensure that the children do not start calling the new partner 'daddy'. If the father has a new partner, the mother may become bitter towards the new partner, as it may be the final realisation that the marriage is over. It is better if the new partner can try and build up a 'working relationship' over the children and reassure the mother that she is not taking her place.

Where there is concern that a child may be abducted by the other parent, or may not be safe with the parent, contact can take place at 'Contact Centres'.

It is preferable for the parents to remain on cordial terms and to co-operate with the other. This includes practical things like sending sensible clothes on a visit. It is beneficial for the children if they are able to do things with both parents, such as having a meal or going on an outing.

It assists if the parent with whom the children live keeps the other parent informed of a child's progress at school by providing copies of school reports and lists of school dates and activities. Where there are specific religious festivals, these should be decided upon and included in the contact arrangements.

Example Alternate Weekend Contact

1 The father have alternate weekend staying contact from 6.00 p.m. Friday to 6.00 p.m. Sunday night.

2 The father to collect and deliver the children.

3 The father to have staying contact to the children of two weeks in the school summer holiday and one week in each of the Christmas and Easter holidays. (Alternate festivals commencing with the mother in 2000.)

4 The father to have a tea contact each Wednesday, collecting the children at 5.00 p.m., and returning them at 7.00 p.m.

5 The father to have telephone contact to the children each Friday.

*Where there are children at school, the tea contact may not be practical with after school events and homework.

Example One Day Each Weekend

Another pattern that can work is:

The father to have the following contact:

1 Weekly staying contact from 6.00 p.m. Friday to 6.00 p.m. Saturday night.

2 The father to have two weeks in the school summer holiday and one week in each of the Christmas and Easter holidays. (Alternate festivals commencing with the mother in 2000.)

*The disadvantage with this pattern is that neither parent has a whole weekend with or without the children.

With older children more complex patterns can work, although they can cause confusion for both the parents and the children.

Example Four Weekly Pattern

The father to have the following contact:

1 Week 1 – Staying contact from 6.00 p.m. Friday to 6.00 p.m. Sunday night.

2 Week 2 – Staying contact from 6.00 p.m. Friday to 6.00 p.m. Saturday night.

3 Week 3 – The father to have no contact.

4 Week 4 – Staying contact from 6.00 p.m. Friday to 6.00 p.m. Saturday night.

5 Two weeks staying contact in the school summer holiday and one week in each of the Christmas and Easter holidays. (Alternate festivals commencing with the mother in 2000).

6 The father to collect and deliver the children.

In some cases, where there is a high degree of co-operation between the parents and both households and the parents are both able to arrange proper child care when the children are with them and have sufficient accommodation, a pattern of shared care can work.

Example Shared Care with Alternate Weeks

1 A joint residency order.

2 Week 1 – 6.00 p.m. Friday to 6.00 p.m. the following Friday children with mother.

3 Week 2 – 6.00 p.m. Friday to 6.00 p.m. the following Friday, children with father.

4 Each parent to have half the school holidays.

5 Alternate Christmas and Easter festivals.

Alternatively:

Example Shared Care with Half a Week Split

1 A joint residency order.

2 Week 1 – 6.00 p.m. Saturday to 6.00 p.m. after school on Wednesday, children with mother.

3 Week 2 – After school on Wednesday to 6.00 p.m. Saturday, children with father.

4 Each parent to have half the school holidays.

5 Alternate Christmas and Easter festivals.

*The disadvantage is that the children move mid-week which can cause problems over moving school uniform and homework.

Specific issues

Where there are particular disputes over the upbringing of a child, an application can be brought to the court on the specific issue. These apply, for example, where the parents cannot decide on the child's religious upbringing or schooling.

Prohibited steps order

An order can be obtained to stop one parent doing something which would be a matter within the ambit of parental responsibility. This can include:

- prohibiting one parent from allowing the child to see a person, deemed unsuitable;
- stopping a parent from exposing the child to an adverse influence such as a religious movement;
- stopping a parent changing a child's education;
- prohibiting a medical treatment the other objects to.

The application can be made as an immediate application (without notice) where necessary. It can be made against a person who does not have parental responsibility, such as a step-parent, who is then given leave to intervene (allowed to participate) in the full proceedings.

Procedure on divorce

The interests of the child are paramount and all matters relating to the children are decided on the basis of what is in the best interests of the child. This is not necessarily what a child says, as children can be influenced by one or other parent. The court's aim is to determine in what environment the child will best thrive. The interests of parents are taken into account but are no longer the most important factor. It is usual for siblings to be kept together.

Under the old law on divorce, the court had to make an order that the arrangements for the children were satisfactory (a section 41 declaration), or 'were not satisfactory but the best in the circumstances'. The decree nisi could not be made absolute until the position with the children had been resolved to the satisfaction of the court. The parent with whom the children were to live had to attend court for a brief interview with the judge and orders for custody, care and control and access were normally made, the usual order being 'joint custody, care and control to mother and reasonable access to the father'.

Under the Children Act 1989, the procedure changed and the current procedures are considered in the context of the divorce procedure (page 34 and below). On divorce, the court will not normally make an order setting out the arrangements for the children.

Court procedure on divorce

On filing the papers for the divorce, the person applying must file a Statement of Arrangement for Children (see page 40). If the respondent disagrees, he can file his own Statement setting out his own proposals. It will be for the court to decide how to deal with the children and if it needs to take any action.

The court may now delay the decree absolute if there are overpowering concerns regarding the children but this is extremely rare and the court must, when considering the making the decree nisi make a declaration stating the following.

- There are no children to whom Matrimonial Causes Act 1973 section 41 applies.
- There is at least one child to whom Matrimonial Causes Act 1973 section 41 applies.

- The court does not need to exercise its powers under the Children Act 1989, nor give a direction under Matrimonial Causes Act 1973 section 41.
- The court does, or may need to, exercise its powers under the Children Act 1989, but there are no exceptional circumstances which make it desirable to give a direction under Matrimonial Causes Act 1973 section 41(2).
- I direct that the decree nisi shall not be made absolute until the court orders otherwise.

If the court does exercise its powers, then it can require that there be a hearing and the procedures as set out below apply.

Effect of court order

Where no specific order is made by the court in respect of parental responsibility, residence and contact, the standard conditions on divorce apply namely:

- Neither parent may change the name of the child until the child attains the age of 18, unless they marry before.
- Neither parent may take the child out of England and Wales.

Procedure if no agreement over child arrangements

Court procedure

If the court, when it considers the divorce petition, is satisfied with the arrangements and does not raise further questions over the children, the parents are still entitled, either before or after the decree nisi, to apply under the Children Act 1989 section 8 for an order as listed above. The application is made on a specific form called a Form C1 in which the child is identified and the parties, and any other person who may have an interest in the child, are set out with a brief statement of the order requested.

The application should be made in the same court as the divorce, although a stand-alone application can be made and under the

Children Act an application in respect of a child can be made in the magistrates court, county court or High Court. It is preferable to proceed in the county court. The courts have the power to transfer the matter between courts and the main criterion is the speed with which the matter can be dealt with.

It is a requirement under the court rules that the court must play an active role in the time tabling of the hearing, and that at each hearing, the next court date must be set. Applications cannot be withdrawn without the agreement of the court and a date for any hearing cannot be adjourned without the court's consent.

Conciliation

The Principal Registry operate a conciliation procedure and in all cases for residence or contact, and those for specific issue or prohibited steps orders (subject to the applicant requesting it), there is a conciliation appointment. The notice for the first appointment will clearly state if it is a conciliation appointment.

In other courts some have a conciliation procedure and the court office of each court can advise of each court's procedures. If there is likely to be a dispute over children, if possible the divorce proceedings should be issued in a court which is convenient to the parties and preferably one operating a conciliation procedure if at all possible.

Where there is a conciliation procedure, a court welfare officer is available at the hearing to talk to the parents and to any child over the age of 10, who should also attend court. The facilities at court are not child friendly and it can help to have a relation or friend present to stay with the child(ren) while the parents are in court. The legal representatives, if there are any, must attend court on a conciliation appointment. The court hearing is relatively short with the basic dispute being outlined to the judge and court welfare officer, and the matter being adjourned so that the welfare officer can talk to the parties and the children. Each court has its own procedures and some welfare officers prefer to speak to both parents together while others speak separately to the parents to ascertain what the dispute is about.

The intention of the hearing is to reach an agreement between the parties with the help of the court welfare officer. What is said to the court welfare officer by the individual parents and the children is confidential. Some officers can be extremely forthright if they feel one or other party is unreasonable. With the help of the court welfare officer and the legal advisers, agreement is frequently achieved by means of a compromise. At the end of the meeting with the court welfare officer, the matter will come back before the district judge and a report on the progress is given. If matters are resolved, an order can be made by consent. A conciliation appointment can be adjourned if need be.

If matters are not agreed, then directions are given for a contested hearing. These will cover the following.

- The exchange of sworn statements by both parents.
- Exchange of questionnaires if appropriate.
- Disclosure of medical records on one of the parents or the child.
- Arrangement for separate examination of one party by a doctor, if applicable.
- If there is a need for the child or children to be examined by a psychiatrist, a specific order to that end.
- That a court welfare officer provide a report to the court and whether he or she should attend the hearing.
- The preparation of the court bundle (i.e. documents for the hearing).
- A timetable for the carrying out of the various steps.
- The next court hearing date.

The next hearing can be either for further directions or for a full hearing. Some courts list a short appointment a few weeks before a final hearing to make sure the case is ready.

The district judge and court welfare officer who have been involved in the conciliation appointment are debarred from being involved in any contested hearing of the matter.

Statements

Depending on the practice of the individual court, statements are filed by the interested parties, usually the parents, either simultaneously, or the applicant first, followed by the respondent, and there should be leave for each party to reply to the allegations made against them. It is also important to set out all the matters complained of in the first statement, and to ensure that the language used is not too emotive. It is important that the parties do not use this process as a means of being vindictive against the other parent. Only matters which can be substantiated should be raised, otherwise it reflects badly on the person raising the issue.

If there are to be other witnesses called, they too should provide statements.

The statement must be dated and signed by the person making it and contain a declaration that:

> 'I believe the statement to be true and that I understand that it may be placed before the court.'

The statement should also have in the top right-hand corner the following.

■ The initials and surname of the person making the statement.

■ The number of the statement in relation to the maker of the statement, i.e. first, second etc.

■ The date when made.

■ The party on whose behalf the statement is filed.

Court welfare officer's report

If a court welfare officer's report is required, the following information should be given.

■ Full names of the children.

■ Their address and telephone number.

■ Details of the parent with whom they live.

■ The name and addresses of schools they attend.

■ Details of their doctor.

■ Details of any other court hearings in which they have been involved.

■ Any special health or educational needs.

■ Any other particular matters which are relevant.

The papers will be sent to the local court welfare office (or the most convenient to where the children are living) and the court welfare officer assigned will arrange to interview both parents and the children. The officers sometimes see the parents together and sometimes separately. They should observe the children with both parents in their own homes and may also require that the children are taken to their office to be interviewed. Where the children are abroad, arrangements can be made for the children to be interviewed wherever they are.

The court welfare officer will obtain reports from the children's schools (which should include details of child's progress, absences and lateness) and, if relevant, the doctor. If the court welfare officer considers that there are matters which give rise for concern, he or she can bring in Social Services to investigate any such concern. These include inappropriate parenting skills, suspected child abuse and neglect.

The welfare report should set out the result of his or her findings, including details of the accommodation each parent has available and the relationship the children have with both parents, and may make recommendations to the court. Any recommendation is not binding on the court but is usually followed by the judge.

The court welfare report is headed with a rider stating that the contents of the report is confidential. This means the contents must not be disclosed to anyone who is not a party to the proceedings or their legal advisers.

Court hearing

Because of the hostility which inevitably arises on a contested hearing, the court is far less inclined to make orders for joint residence, since it is apparent that the parties are unable to co-operate with each other.

A hearing takes place usually before a district or circuit judge but can be heard by a High Court judge.

The court at the directions hearing sets a time estimate for the hearing. If the time estimate changes, it is necessary to advise the court immediately. If the time estimate increases the court may have to adjourn the original date to a date when a judge is available. It is not desirable to start a case, knowing that it will have to adjourn 'part heard' as it can take between three to six months to be heard again.

A court bundle will need preparing and the directions will set out on whom the obligation lies to prepare the bundle. It is usually the applicant, but increasingly the obligation is placed equally on both parties. The directions quite often require the court bundle to be lodged with the court in advance of the hearing.

The documents are put in a paginated bundle consisting of the following:

- application;
- any orders or directions;
- statements filed by both parties, in date order;
- court welfare officer's report (and any supplementary reports);
- any medical reports, doctor's notes, etc;
- any other evidence.

One copy of the bundle is needed for the judge and the witnesses and each party should have a copy.

The court directions will deal with whether the court welfare officer should attend the hearing. Frequently the direction will state that the court welfare officer should attend unless given a week's notice that his or her attendance is not required. Directions such as that should be adhered to strictly.

The courts are increasingly making a direction that a chronology be filed with the court and even if there is no direction to this effect, a chronology should be prepared setting out the important dates in the case and the significant facts.

If case law is to be referred to, a list of cases with their references should be given to the court in advance of the hearing, and in the county court, copies of the actual case reports should be brought for use of the court. The case details should be given to the other party before the hearing.

At the hearing, the applicant will set out the background to the case and, as in financial relief applications, a chronology is frequently used. The applicant's evidence is given and his or her witnesses are called. Each witness may be cross-examined by the other party and the judge may also ask questions. Once the applicant's case is completed, the respondent will present his or her case in the same way.

The court will hear evidence from the court welfare officer at a convenient moment. If there are expert witnesses, the judge will sometimes allow them to give evidence at a time convenient to them.

These proceedings take place 'in camera' (in private) so that anyone who is not involved in the proceedings, may not be present in court without the agreement of the judge.

After the evidence the respondent sums up the evidence and then the applicant gives the 'closing speech'. Judgement can be given immediately, but if there are difficult issues, it can be given later, either by post or by a short further appointment being fixed.

In children's cases, usually there is no order for costs between the parties. If, however, one party has conducted the matter in a way which is unreasonable, the court can order them to pay the costs. See costs section generally, page 159.

Can a child be represented?

Occasionally, a child may wish to express his or her own view to the court, and a child can be a party to the proceedings if the court agrees or a solicitor is prepared to act for the child. The solicitor should be a specialist and preferably a member of the Law Society's Children's Panel.

Alternatively, if proceedings need to be brought by a child, the child can be represented by his or her 'next friend', which can include a parent or, if the dispute is with the parent, a third party. Where a child is a defendant to proceedings, he or she can be represented by a 'guardian *ad litem*' who can be a professional guardian. Both 'next friends' and 'guardians' can be the official solicitor whose job it is to represent the interests of persons unable to represent themselves.

Taking the child out of the jurisdiction

If the parent, for example the mother, with whom the child resides, wants to move abroad permanently, she must have the court's permission to take the child abroad. If the other parent agrees, the application is straightforward and the mother must give the court a formal undertaking (promise) to 'return the children to the jurisdiction if called upon to do so'.

If the other parent objects to the removal, the court will have to decide whether it is reasonable for the mother to go abroad with the child. The relevant factors are as follows.

- Is there a good reason for the mother going abroad? If the mother intends an itinerant lifestyle, the court would not consider this appropriate.
- Has she a family attachment with the country she is going to?
- Is she accompanying her new partner?
- Are there half-brothers and half-sisters from a new relationship, and would the relationship with these children be effected by the separation?
- Has the mother considered the financial needs of herself and the child and can she get gainful employment?
- Has the mother considered the educational needs of the child, and are there appropriate schools for the child to attend offering a suitable type of education? In many countries British and International schools are available. Will the child be educated in an English speaking school or a school teaching in a language which is known to the child?
- What will be the effect on the relationship with the father? It is inevitable that there will be less contact with the father as a result of the move abroad. What can be done to minimise the reduction of contact?
- What is the father's relationship with the child, and how will this be affected by the separation?
- Has the father's contact with the child settled into a

new pattern following the divorce? Would a delay in the move help the father's relationship develop?

■ What would be the effect on the mother if the court refused leave to take the child abroad, would she go anyway and leave the child or would she remain to be with the child, but be so resentful that it would be to the child's detriment to stop the mother taking the child?

■ Are there now or shortly to be new half siblings?

■ Can the child's cultural links with the other parent's background be maintained?

Specimen 'Minute of Agreement' for the Mother to Take the Child Abroad Permanently

AND UPON THE FATHER AND MOTHER AGREEING:

1 To exercise joint parental responsibility.

2 That the father will meet the costs of air travel to and from to include the costs of the child (and the mother in the event she accompanies the child) and that such costs will be treated as a prior deduction in calculating the father's eligible income in respect of an application of financial relief. Further the father and mother will make available a minimum of 50% of their air miles in any year to defray the cost of air tickets.

AND UPON THE MOTHER AGREEING:

3 To make the travel arrangements to and from _____ the mother delivering and collecting the child to and from the jurisdiction, unless agreed otherwise, it being agreed that the father will meet the cost of airfares.

4 That she will ensure that the said child should continue to maintain contact with her English background and culture and will attend an English speaking school or nursery or a school where there is adequate English teaching, unless agreed otherwise in writing by the father.

IT IS ORDERED THAT:

1 That A (the child) do reside with their mother.

2 The mother do have leave to remove the child from the jurisdiction to reside in (Town, Province, Country).

3 The mother do permit the father to have contact with the child as follows:

   (a) No less than two weeks staying contact and not more than half the summer school holiday on dates to be agreed between the parties, a minimum of two weeks to be taken consecutively.

   (b) One week staying contact at each of the Christmas and Easter holidays, in England, with alternate Christmas and New Year festivals and the father having alternate Easter.

   (c) Visiting contact during the school term-time to the father to include the following:

      i)   That the father should have a long weekend with the child in England over each half-term and/or bank/public holiday.

      ii) One other weekend contact each half-term from Friday night to Sunday night.

   (d) Such other contact as may be agreed between the parties

   (e) That the father do have telephone contact to the said child twice a week at such times as may be agreed between the parties, when the child is with her mother and the mother do have telephone contact to the said child twice a week at such times as may be agreed between the parties, when the child is with the father for a period of a week or more.

4 That in accordance with section 11(7) (b) of the Children Act 1989, the following conditions shall apply:

   (a) That the mother will return the child to England and Wales when called upon to do so.

   (b) That the mother will make all necessary arrangements to ensure that the child boards the appropriate flights and will accompany the child, or arrange for the child to be accompanied by an appropriate adult on the flights and will deliver her to the father at the airport for contact and will collect the child from the father at the airport at the end of the visit.

(c) That the mother will keep the father notified of all school dates, school events and will provide copies of all communications received by her in respect of the said child's school including school reports.

(d) That the mother will give notice of any proposed changes in respect of her residence and in respect of any changes in respect of the child's schooling, such notice to be given at least one term in advance, unless the circumstances are such that such notice is not possible, in which case she will give as much notice as is possible.

(e) That the mother will consult the father fully in respect of any changes in the school the said child shall attend from time to time.

(f) That the mother will provide the father with full details of the said child's doctor and dentist, and will keep the father advised of any illness, medical or dental treatment undertaken by the said child and save for an emergency, consult the father in advance of treatment.

5 There be liberty to both parties to apply.

Dated this day ____ of ____.

Wardship

This is a rare procedure in private law cases (i.e. within the family) and is appropriate where there is an urgent need to protect the child. The court has power under statute to make such orders where the child is:

- Habitually resident in England and Wales.
- Present in England and Wales but not habitually resident in England and Wales.
- Is present in England and Wales and the court considers that the immediate exercise of its power's is necessary for the child's protection.

■ Under its 'inherent power' (the historic obligation to protect a child) to make an order which applies:

– to any British subject under the age of 18;

– whether resident or present in England and Wales;

– domiciled here;

– or habitually resident or ordinarily resident in England and Wales.

(In this later case, if the child is not physically present in England and Wales, the court must consider what the court would do where the child is.)

The application is made to the Family Division of the High Court and the child becomes a ward immediately the application is filed.

The following documents are filed.

■ Application in a prescribed form called an 'Originating Summons'.

■ Certified copy of birth certificate or copy of entry in the Adoption Children Register.

■ Court fee (see page 183).

The defendant (the other party) is usually the other parent, but if the issue is to stop the child seeing another person, then that person is the defendant.

The Originating Summons is served on the defendant who must file an 'Acknowledgement of Service' (confirmation that he has received the papers) with the court within 14 days.

A first appointment must be taken out within 21 days of lodging the original papers, or else the application lapses.

The application will be listed for a first appointment and the procedure will be similar to that set out above under the Children Act. See page 143.

If there is no-one else available, such as a parent to represent the view of the child, the official solicitor can be appointed to represent the child.

Wardship will continue until the child reaches the age of 18 unless ended earlier. Once a child is a ward of court, the court has parental responsibility and the following matters require the court's consent.

- Any psychiatric examination of the child.
- Marriage by the ward.
- Adoption.
- Taking the child out of England and Wales.
- Publishing any information relating to the child. (However, consent is usually given if a child is missing with a view to finding the child.)

The Court's powers include the following.

- Making 'a care and control order' in favour of a parent or a third party, such as a grandparent or foster parent. (A parental responsibility order cannot be made as the court has parental responsibility.)
- Make 'contact orders' so that the child can maintain contact with both parents.
- Make residence orders which include, if appropriate, permitting the child's removal from England and Wales.
- Make financial provision for the child.
- Decisions about the religious upbringing.
- Decisions about what education the child should receive and which school he or she should attend.

The court has immediate powers to make orders to protect the child and this includes making orders so that the child is not allowed to leave the country, which can be notified to the passport authorities at the airports. If the whereabouts of the child are unknown, the court can order anyone with information regarding the whereabouts of the child to give that information to the court. The court has powers to make orders to ensure compliance of the order which can include instructing the Tipstaff (a court official whose job it is to ensure that court orders are complied with and he or she in turn can bring in the police).

If a person breaches a wardship order, that person is in contempt of court and the court will not usually hear any application until the contempt has been 'purged', i.e. the order complied with.

Child abduction

When a child is taken out of England and Wales by one parent, without the agreement of the other parent, this can be abduction. By international law, some countries in particular European countries and some states in the United States, have agreed a procedure for the return of such children, when asked by another court to assist.

The criterion is that the child should be returned to the country of 'habitual residence' (where he or she lived immediately before the abduction). An application must quickly be made to the court in the country where the child has been taken.

Parentage

Sometimes a father will dispute that he is the biological father of a child. This is relevant to the question of child support (since only the biological parent is obliged to maintain a child) and to the question of whether a child is a child of the family. If the father treated the child as his own child, without knowing that it is not his, the court may take that fact into account.

If there is a dispute over parentage, it is possible to have blood tests carried out on both the child, mother and putative father. While the analysis used to be by blood group, DNA profiling gives a much more accurate analysis and can be determined from a blood sample.

The blood sample is sent to a DNA testing laboratory where it is analysed. The findings can show whether the putative father is the biological father.

If agreement for the tests to be carried out is not forthcoming, the court has the power to order that blood samples are given so that DNA tests can be carried out.

5 | **COSTS**

This Chapter sets out the different considerations on costs, whether between the solicitor and the client or the parties themselves. It also covers legal aid.

What are costs?

When referring to costs there are different aspects, for example, those due to a person's own solicitor, and those that are incurred in the litigation by the one party and which may be recoverable from the other party.

Solicitor's costs

When a person instructs a solicitor, he or she agrees to pay the solicitor fees for the work he or she carries out, 'solicitor and client costs'. Solicitors are required by the Law Society (the professional body) to set out the terms and conditions he or she works under. These include keeping the client informed of the way the charges are calculated, the hourly rate for the work done and the amount of the costs as they are incurred.

Solicitors have standard terms under which they work, and details are provided to a client at the commencement of the action. These terms become a contract and the client is obliged to pay the solicitor's costs in any event and irrespective of whether any costs are recovered from the other party.

The solicitor's costs should reflect the importance of the work to the client, the skill required, the experience of the person doing the work and the time involved. It was usual for an hourly rate (the amount charged per hour of time spent on a matter, including telephone calls, preparing letters, court documents, attending court, travelling and seeing the client) to be quoted with an additional item for 'care and attention' to reflect the complexity of a matter, etc. Now it is usual to quote an all-inclusive hourly rate.

The solicitor is entitled to exercise 'a lien over the papers' (keep the client's papers) until paid in full for the work done.

The client is entitled to have the costs checked to make sure they are not excessive. In the case of a matter which has not gone to court, the Law Society can assess the costs. Where there are court proceedings, the court can determine whether the costs are reasonable.

Rarely, an order for costs can be made against a solicitor personally to pay the other party's costs (see page 162).

Costs orders between the parties

The costs in respect of each aspect of the divorce are dealt with separately, so that the costs of the petition, the financial relief application and the children are treated within the individual applications.

The costs orders made by the court are:

■ 'No order for costs', where each party pays its own costs. This is used frequently where one party has made an application and not been successful in full.

■ 'One party pay the costs of the other' where the unsuccessful party will have to pay the costs either as assessed at the hearing or as later determined by an assessment (see page 163). This can be made in respect of individual applications such as an application for maintenance pending suit, or in respect of the whole action.

■ 'Costs in the application' (or 'costs in the cause'), where the costs of both parties in respect of the application will roll up and form part of the costs of the whole matter, when determined at the end and the costs of this hearing will be included in the costs paid to the successful party.

■ 'Costs reserved', where the court cannot determine on the information before it who should pay the costs and they are then determined at the next hearing. This type of order is frequently used when there is an urgent application to the court and the court has only heard one party's case.

Costs on the divorce petition

Usually the respondent pays the costs of the divorce, particularly if it is based on adultery or behaviour. These will be defined as the petitioner's 'standard costs' which are a few hundred pounds and are usually agreed.

Sometimes if a petition is agreed, one party may object to paying the costs and the other may agree to not ask for them, to avoid a dispute.

If costs cannot be agreed the court can decide who should pay (see page 43).

Costs in respect of children's applications

Usually each party should pay their own costs as the prime aim of the litigation is to find the best solution for the children and accordingly neither party should be penalised. The court can order costs if it considers one party has acted unreasonably or extended the litigation unnecessarily. The effect of legal aid is frequently relevant to the question of costs, see below.

Costs in respect of the financial claim

The general rule in litigation is that the successful party should receive their costs on a 'standard basis' from the unsuccessful party, i.e. 'costs follow the event'. This principle does apply in family cases particularly in financial proceedings but the court has a broad discretion over costs. Changes made in 1999 following the Woolf reforms (named after Lord Woolf) provide that the court must take account of the following.

■ The conduct of the parties. This includes the way the litigation has been conducted, for example, Has it been excessively aggressive, both before the case started and after? Have there been attempts to settle matters, or has one party hidden assets? It will also include whether the party was reasonable to pursue an enquiry, whether the manner has been appropriate, and the extent of the success.

■ Whether a party has been successful in part or all. The court will take an overview. If one party is seeking £500,000 and gets £100,000 then that party has not been successful. If another person seeks £80,000 and gets £75,000 they have been successful.

■ Whether any reasonable offer has been made. The court, once it has determined the case, should consider any offers to settle. This includes any 'Calderbank offers', 'part 36 offers', or correspondence which is 'without prejudice save as to costs'. The court will deal with costs on the basis of whether a party has 'beaten' the Calderbank, i.e. offered the other party more than the court has ordered.

If the situation is that the court has ordered less than the wife wanted but more than the husband offered, the costs are entirely at the discretion of the court.

■ Proportionality, i.e. are the costs incurred reasonable in the context of the overall assets and the benefit derived from their being incurred? The judge can also order a higher rate of statutory interest where he considers the conduct of one of the parties inappropriate.

Normally, the matrimonial assets will be used to pay the costs of both parties, although there are certainly situations where, if one party has incurred costs unnecessarily, he or she may have to pay the costs, or not obtain a costs order in their favour. As the wife with dependant children has a basic need for housing for herself and the children, it is the husband who will receive the balance of the assets, once the wife's needs is met. As the costs are met out of the residue and it is in the husband's interest to keep the costs down.

There are further changes in respect of costs which will apply after June 2000 (see page 177).

Procedure in respect of costs

At each hearing, in respect of a financial relief application, the solicitor must advise the court what the costs are at that point and provide a costs schedule. There are obligations to provide written costs estimates at all financial hearings under the Pilot Scheme. Under the Woolf reforms, the court on each application must deal with costs and make an order for costs. From June 2000 the costs estimates are to be in a prescribed form.

If one party wants an order for costs on an interim application, such as an application for maintenance pending suit, or an injunction, the party must serve on the other details of their costs 24 hours before the hearing. The judge can then order a specific sum be paid rather than an 'order for assessment'.

Specifically, under the Pilot Scheme, the costs of the first appointment and financial dispute appointment are dealt with as 'costs in the application', if the matter proceeds to a full hearing.

At the conclusion of the final hearing, the judge, once judgment is given, will decide who should pay the costs. It is at this point that any offers to settle, made either before or after the proceedings started, and whether sent as open offers, 'without prejudice save as to costs' offers (otherwise called 'Calderbank offers'), or 'part 36 offers', are produced. The court may be aware of the open offers before deciding the case, but will see the 'without prejudice' offers for the first time at this point.

The judge will take into account whether a reasonable offer has been made and the court can award the costs of one party up to the date of the offer (or a reasonable period after to allow time for consideration), and then not allow the costs after that date. The court can award a percentage of the costs to reflect the behaviour of one party in respect of the litigation or costs between particular dates or stages in the litigation.

Where the court decides one party has behaved unreasonably in respect of the conduct of the proceedings it can award penalty interest. The court also at this point will consider any 'reserved orders' for costs.

A party who receives money by way of a settlement should remember that the solicitor is entitled to take out of any monies he or she receives on the client's behalf his or her billed costs, provided he or she has submitted an account and it has been agreed. This can cause an immediate shortfall in the amount available to the wife to rehouse herself and the children. There can also be similar difficulties where a party is legally aided and is awarded a lump sum to rehouse herself as a result of the statutory charge, although it should be possible to avoid this (see page 170).

The type of costs orders defined

The normal basis for costs is the 'standard' basis, i.e. those costs between the parties which the other should pay. On this basis they will be proportionate to the whole issue. Any dispute over the actual amount of any costs that are payable will be decided in favour of the party paying the costs.

Indemnity costs are rarely ordered and only because the court wishes to penalise a party for their conduct or handling of the matter. This can include where one party makes allegations which are totally unreasonable and, instead of withdrawing them at an appropriate point, persists in the allegation. It can be where the lawyers have not conducted the matter properly, such as failing to turn up at court for a hearing. Where there is a dispute over the actual amount of the costs, the dispute is resolved in favour of the receiving party.

Where there has been misconduct, i.e. one party has behaved unreasonably in respect of the application, the court can disallow part or all of the person's costs or penalise him or her by awarding costs against him or her.

In some situations costs orders can be made against the solicitor or barrister personally, called 'a wasted costs order', and if a person has legal aid, against the Legal Aid Board. Such orders are very rare and are appropriate where the lawyer has acted improperly, unreasonably or negligently. The lawyer has the right to make representations to the court over the liability to pay. There can be difficulties over confidentiality if a solicitor is opposing the costs order against him or herself because he or she may have to bring in matters involving his or her client.

Costs in favour of a 'litigant in person' (a person acting with no solicitor) can be ordered and a litigant in person can recover an element for the time spent by him on the matter up to two thirds of the amount a solicitor would have charged.

Procedure on assessment of costs

Following the implementation of the Woolf reforms, the court must decide who should pay on each application, i.e. assess the costs of the application or order the costs to be in the cause (or the application). When the matter is concluded and the final costs order is made, if the costs are not determined ('a summary assessment'), i.e. quantified at the hearing (and it is intended under the new procedures that the court will assess the costs on hearings lasting under a day), then there will be an order for a detailed assessment of costs.

The person in whose favour the costs are awarded must prepare and serve on the other side within three months the following.

- A 'notice of commencement of the costs procedure' in a prescribed form.
- 'Detailed assessment', which is a detailed statement setting out the work done, the charging rates used, the disbursements (for example, fares, counsel's fees, court fees and experts fees). It is a specialist job to prepare the bill and the papers are usually sent to a costs draughtsman to prepare.
- Copies of counsel and expert's fee notes.
- Written evidence of any disbursement over £250.
- Statement giving the name and address of anyone on whom the bill is to be served.

The paying party must serve 'points of dispute' setting out the objections to any item of costs claimed within 21 days. If no points of dispute are served, the party whose costs they are may apply for a 'default costs certificate'. If points of dispute are filed, the party whose costs they are may file a reply within 21 days and must then file with the court a request for a detailed assessment hearing.

If the person whose costs they are fails to file a request for a detailed statement, the paying party can apply for an order that he or she does so and conditions can be imposed by the court.

The procedure is the same as set out where the party is legally aided (see page 171).

When the court has determined the costs, an order is made and this is enforceable in the same way as a judgement debt. Interest is due on any outstanding costs from the date the costs order is made.

Legal aid

Legal aid is a system whereby the Legal Aid Board meets the legal costs of the party and if as a result of the litigation any money or property is awarded or preserved, the costs are repaid out of the property awarded. Effectively it amounts in many cases to a loan.

The advantage to the legally aided person is that the costs charged by the solicitor are lower than the amount normally charged as there are prescribed charging rates for family work and the costs are scrutinised by the court.

From 2000, only firms who have the appropriate authorisation from the Legal Aid Board can undertake matrimonial cases. Each firm who does legal aid work will have a legal aid account number allocated to it which must be quoted on all applications and claims for costs. Each legal aid certificate is issued to a named solicitor and any solicitor acting must have a current practising certificate and they are identified by their Law Society roll number.

A legal aid certificate can be transferred from one solicitor's firm to another, but a reason must be given for the change and if there are a number of changes, the Legal Aid Board can refuse the change, in particular if the additional expense caused by the change cannot be justified.

Legal aid is available to people living abroad in respect of proceedings in England and Wales, but is not available in respect of proceedings being conducted abroad.

Legal aid will only cover work within the terms for which it is granted and for work done after it is granted. Legal aid can never be retrospective.

A solicitor cannot demand payment from a client when there is a valid legal aid certificate in force.

Types of legal aid

'Advice and assistance' (sometimes called the Green Form scheme) applies where there are uncontested divorce proceedings and a 'form of application' is completed; and the contribution is calculated by the solicitor. There is a ceiling on the value of the work that can be done, limited to three hours work by the solicitor, although extensions can be obtained. Where a solicitor prepares a petition under the Green Form scheme, the assisted person must sign the form and can include his/her address as 'care of' the solicitor. Only if a petition is defended may legal aid be available to cover the costs of the defended action, but the Legal Aid Board is reluctant to fund a contested divorce.

Legal aid is available for a financial application in respect of the children and injunctions, whether financial or for non-molestation. For some applications concerning children, legal aid is automatically available to the children. Composite legal aid certificates are usually granted and a certificate can be extended to cover related litigation as a matter progresses. Where the statutory charge applies in a case, it covers all the costs incurred under a certificate, for example, where a certificate covers both a child dispute and the financial application.

Emergency legal aid is available if legal action needs to be taken urgently and an application can be faxed to the Legal Aid Board and can be granted over the telephone. The application papers must still be completed and submitted to the Legal Aid Board in such circumstances.

Eligibility

For people on limited means and particularly people on state benefit, advice and assistance and legal aid should be available. To be eligible for legal aid, a person's means must fall within the following:

Eligibility for Legal Aid

	Lower limit	Higher limit
Income	£2,723 per annum	£8,067 per annum
Capital	£3,000	£6,750

If a person is under both the lower limit for capital and income, no contribution will be made. If between the lower and higher limits, a contribution will be payable. If a person is over the higher limits, a person will not be eligible.

Any person in receipt of income support or income based jobseeker's allowance will be eligible for legal aid without a contribution.

In calculating the assessable income, an allowance is made for the actual living costs of the applicant.

Where a person has a property with a mortgage, only the first £100,000 of a mortgage is taken into account in the calculation.

Where there are assets which cannot be sold, such as a property which is in joint names with the spouse and which cannot be sold without that person's consent, the value may be left out of account.

While in most cases the joint financial position of a husband and wife are used for calculating eligibility for legal aid, in family cases the means of the spouses are not included.

Method of application

Application for legal aid must be made on the specific form.

The Forms of Application for Legal Aid

- ■ Application form for family cases – Form APP2.
- ■ Financial statement – Form Means 1 for people not receiving state benefit.
- ■ Form Means 2 for people on benefit.
- ■ If a person is in employment, a statement of earnings – Form L17 (signed by the employer).

- If a person is self-employed – Form L18
- If a person is a director of a company – Form L30 (signed by the company accountant).
- If a matter is urgent and an application must be made urgently to the court, an emergency fax application Form APP11 and emergency application of means Form APP11(a) can be faxed to the Legal Aid Board.

The application form requires the full name, address, occupation, telephone number, National Insurance number and date of birth of the person applying for legal aid.

The Legal Aid Board consider the application on its merits, i.e. by assessing whether a person has a reasonable case and on whether the person is financially eligible.

If legal aid is refused, a notice of refusal is issued. There is usually no appeal against an assessment of means or determination of the contribution. There can be an appeal against a refusal on the merits. An appeal to the Area Committee must be lodged within 14 days, in writing. The appeal can be conducted either on the basis of written representation or on the basis of a hearing before the appeal tribunal.

Once legal aid is granted, the certificate and any amendments must be filed with the court in which the proceedings are proceeding. Notice of issue of legal aid, and in the event of an amendment a 'notice of amendment of legal aid', must be served on the other party and filed with the court.

Conditions are frequently applied to any grant of legal aid such as a maximum figure for costs which can be incurred. These conditions must be strictly adhered to.

Obligations of a legally assisted person

When legal aid is granted, the assisted person (someone in receipt of legal aid) is obliged to advise the Legal Aid Board of the following.

- Any change in their address.

■ If they remarry (as legal aid is assessed on the assets of the husband and wife, unless the spouse is the opposite party in the litigation).

■ Any change in their income or capital position.

Where there is a change in the person's financial position, the Legal Aid Board will reassess the person's eligibility for legal aid. If a person is then not eligible, the legal aid certificate will be discharged. The position is that the work carried out under the certificate will be met by the Legal Aid Board, but future costs will not be.

In certain circumstances, for example, where the assisted person has been uncooperative, legal aid may be revoked. This means the legal aid is deemed never to have existed and the Legal Aid Board will pay the solicitors' their costs but can recover the amount of costs from the assisted person.

There is an obligation on the assisted person to act reasonably. Where a reasonable offer of settlement is made, the obligation is to accept the offer. If the lawyer advises that a settlement is reasonable, if the assisted person does not agree to accept the offer, then the solicitor is obliged to notify the Legal Aid Board, and the Board is likely to terminate the certificate. If the Board are minded to discharge the certificate, they will notify the assisted person and the solicitor.

Effect of legal aid

If a person has legal aid there are a number of effects in respect of the conduct of the proceedings which will effect the other party. They are as follows.

■ For the period during which a party has legal aid, the court can order that he or she pay the costs of the other party, but the costs cannot be enforced until the court has assessed his or her ability to pay the costs.

■ Where one party has legal aid and the other has not, the court is reluctant to order the legally aided person to pay the costs of the non-legally aided person, unless the conduct of the litigation warrants it. It is becoming more frequently the view that the non-legally aided person should bear all the costs of the action.

- Because a costs order against a legally aided person is frequently meaningless if he or she does not have the money to pay the costs, and if the conduct of the matter has been such that no reasonable person would have conducted the litigation, an order for costs against the Legal Aid Board can be asked for. The Board has the right to be represented and such applications are extremely rare.

- Because of the effect of the Family Law Act 1996 section 29, which came into force during 1999, where a person is eligible for legal aid, before a legal aid certificate is issued, he or she must be invited to attend an information meeting with his or her spouse and be assessed for whether he or she should have mediation to try to resolve the issues. If the person is either not considered suitable for mediation, for example, the spouse is violent, or the non-legally aided person refuses to attend, then full legal aid should be granted. If, however, the applicant refuses to attend the meeting, then a full legal aid certificate may not be granted.

- Where an order for costs is made against the husband or wife, the costs are determined at the standard rate, which is approximately double the prescribed rate. In effect it is the solicitor who will benefit from the costs order, rather than the assisted person.

- Where a person is in receipt of legal aid, he or she cannot be required to pay any money to the solicitor for the work covered by the certificate.

- Where a party has legal aid, any monies ordered to be paid must be made to the solicitor or to the Legal Aid Board, i.e. not to the assisted person.

- The solicitor has a duty to the Legal Aid Board which includes an obligation to protect the legal aid funds and not to compromise the position of the Legal Aid Board, for example, in respect of negotiating a compromise.

Statutory charge

Where a person 'preserves' (keeps property claimed by the other in the application), or recovers (is awarded money or property) as a result of the proceedings, the statutory charge applies except for the first £2,500 of money or property preserved or recovered and any maintenance payment for the spouse and children.

The solicitor is obliged to pay any money received to the Legal Aid Board. In practice, a solicitor will pay a sum estimated to cover the costs liability to the Legal Aid Board and having got the Board's consent, release the balance to the assisted person. Once the assessment of costs is dealt with, the Legal Aid Board sends the balance of the monies received to the assisted person, after allowing for any contributions from the assisted person, the money paid in and interest accrued on those monies less the amount of the costs.

If property (for example land) is preserved or awarded, the statutory charge applies to the property and the statutory charge is secured against the property by a charge. If it is land, a charge is registered at the Land Registry. The solicitor must notify the Legal Aid Board on Form Admin 1. Where a charge against property is given, statutory interest is charged on an annual basis currently of 8% on the amount due to the Legal Aid Board. While there is no obligation to repay either the interest or capital until the property is sold, the rate of interest is currently uncompetitive as against mortgage rate. Although it may be helpful in the short-term to have the loan (and it is certainly better than not having the money to invest in a house), it should be viewed as a short-term loan and repaid at the earliest opportunity.

If either money is ordered to be paid to buy a house or the former matrimonial home is ordered to be transferred to the legally aided person for the provision of a home, the court order must provide for a postponement of the order by including the following wording. In addition, an application must be made to the Legal Aid Board for their consent to the postponement.

Example Wording for Postponement of Statutory Charge

Clause where there is a lump sum order:

It is hereby certified for the purpose of the Civil Legal Aid (General) Regulations 1989 that the lump sum of £ _____ has been ordered to be paid to enable the petitioner/respondent to purchase a home for his/herself [and his/her dependants].

Or where property retained:

It is hereby certified for the purposes of the Civil Legal Aid (General) Regulations 1989 that the property namely [_____] has been preserved/recovered for the petitioner/respondent for use as a home him/her [and his/her dependants].

Assessment of costs

Once the matter is completed, the final order should provide for the assessment of costs under the legal aid regulations.

A 'detailed assessment' will need preparation and the papers will need to be sent to a costs draughtsman, as the preparation of the assessment is a special skill. The detailed assessment sets out the history of the matter, the charging rates used, the work done, broken down by letters received, letters written, telephone calls, personal attendances and includes the expenses including counsel's fees and items of expenditure incurred in relation to the matter.

If more than one firm of solicitors have acted, the final solicitor to act deals with the taxation for all the previous firms and each firm should approve and sign their part of the bill before it is lodged with the court.

Where the assisted person is going to have to pay part of the costs, i.e. the statutory charge applies, the solicitor must send the assisted person a copy of the detailed assessment and advise them that they have the right to attend on the taxation and should reply within 14 days.

The detailed assessment includes a statement that the assisted person has or has not an interest in the taxation, and whether the former has been served with a copy and has or has not indicated they wish to attend on the taxation.

The detailed assessment must be signed by a partner in the firm of solicitors and is filed with the court with a court fee of £80. Some courts require all the papers filed separated as correspondence, court documents, counsel's papers, invoices, legal aid certificates.

The court will either:

■ Make a 'provisional assessment' whereby the taxing officer or district judge will check the papers and approve the costs. If he or she disagrees with a profit cost item, he or she will write the amount by which he or she 'disallows' the figure in the left-hand column. If it is a disbursement, he or she will strike through the figure in the second right-hand column and add the figure he or she allows.

If the solicitor does not agree the figures, he or she can require an appointment before the court.

The court returns the detailed assessment to the solicitor who must notify any barrister within 14 days if the barristers fees have been reduced.

■ Set a date for the taxation of costs when the solicitor whose bill it is must attend. If the bill includes costs against the other party, the other party or his solicitors and the person whose costs it is, if that person has an interest in the outcome. After the taxation the detailed assessment is given to the solicitor to 'make up'.

The solicitor then 'makes up' the bill by completing the figures. The detailed assessment must again be signed by the solicitor. If there are any specific queries raised by the judge, they must be dealt with and frequently include the need to 'vouch' the expenditure, i.e. file with the court invoices to show the expenditure.

The detailed assessment is then lodged with the court. It is important that a copy of the completed detailed assessment is retained by the solicitor as it will need to be sent to the Legal Aid Board. Some courts require that the solicitor lodges the 'allocatur' – the court's determination of the costs – whereas other courts prepare their own allocatur.

When the allocatur is received, it, and a copy of the detailed assessment, are sent to the Legal Aid Board, together with the Legal Aid Board Form Claim 1. Once the Legal Aid Board authorises payment of the legal aid, the copy detailed assessment is returned to the solicitor.

Sometimes the other party will pay the full amount of the legally aided person's costs, in which case the Legal Aid Board is notified that no claim will be made for costs using Form Claim 2.

6 | CHANGES IN THE LAW

This Chapter sets out the various announced changes in the law or procedure, which may or may not take place at some future date.

New divorce procedure

The Family Law Act 1996 was made law in 1996 and the new divorce process had been expected to be brought into effect in December 2000. Trials have been running, and following an announcement on the 17 June 1999, the implementation has been delayed, possibly indefinitely. A new announcement is due in the summer 2000 when the act will either be introduced, amended or possibly cancelled.

The new law regime will provide for 'divorce over time'. The process will require that the parties are given information on the consequences of divorce and will encourage the parties to see mediators and counsellors to try and save the marriage.

The scheme in its present form is set out on page 47.

The nationwide 'Pilot Scheme'

The Pilot Scheme in respect of financial relief proceedings (see page 74) is to be introduced nationwide as from 5th June 2000 when the Family Proceedings (Amendment No 2) Rules 1999 come into force. The present scheme as outlined is amended with an overriding objective which is:

■ to ensure that the parties are on an equal footing;

■ saving expense;

■ deal with the case in a way which is proportionate to

the amount of money involved, the importance of the case, complexity and the financial position of each party;

- ■ to ensure dealt with expeditiously and fairly;
- ■ allotting to it a fair share of the court's resources.

The parties must help the court in this objective and the court must encourage the parties to co-operate with each other and to settle their disputes.

The court is to limit the extent of disclosure of documents and expert evidence. All financial applications will commence with a Form A and if there is to be a claim on a pension scheme, the terms of the order requested must be included. A modified Form E will be used as a sworn statement to which should be attached those of the prescribed documents which are relevant.

Prescribed Documents to be Attached to Form E

1 A valuation of the matrimonial home or other property, if obtained within the last 6 months

2 Bank statements for each bank account, for the last 12 months

3 Any surrender values in respect of any life insurance policies

4 The last two years accounts in respect of any business interest or other document on which a capital value of a business is based

5 The last three payslips and the P60 for the last financial year

6 If self-employed or in partnership, the accounts for the last two financial years.

A modified timetable is introduced including additional documents to be served fourteen days before the first appointment.

Timetable Under the Nationwide Scheme

■ **Week 1**

File application for financial relief in Form A with the court. Court sets first appointment date within 12–16 weeks. Within 4 days serve application on respondent.

Serve the application on mortgagees, trustees and pension trustees where appropriate.

■ **Week 7/11**

Five weeks before first appointment – exchange and file sworn Form E (financial statement).

■ **Week 10/14**

Two weeks before first appointment – file and serve:

– a concise statement of issues between the parties;

– a chronology;

– a questionnaire setting out by reference to the concise statement of issues, any further documents or information requested, or a statement that nothing is required;

– Notice in Form G stating whether that party is ready on the first appointment to have a FDR appointment;

– if an order in respect of pensions is sought, confirmation that the pension trustees have been given two weeks notice of the application;

– where the application includes a property adjustment order or a variation of settlement, confirmation that the application has been served on the mortgagees and trustees;

– (before the hearing) file a statement of costs in Form H.

■ **1 week before FDR**

The applicant file details of all offers and counter-offers.

File updated costs schedule in Form H.

On the first appointment the court must:

■ decide what questions must be answered and documents produced;

■ give directions about valuations of assets;

– expert evidence

– what other evidence is required including chronologies and schedules.

- direct that an FDR take place unless a referral is not appropriate, in which case one of the following is ordered;
  - a further directions appointment
  - a hearing of an interim order
  - a final hearing
  - adjournment for an out of court mediation or private negotiations or where there are exceptional circumstances.
- order costs.

and may;

- make an interim order if an application is made 14 days in advance;
- use the first appointment as a FDR;
- if a claim made for a pension, order either party to get a valuation from the pension trustees.

At the FDR appointment, the district judge will try and assist the parties reach agreement, and he will not be involved in any further part of the proceedings if the matter proceeds to a contested hearing. If a settlement is reached a consent order is entered into. If it does not settle the matter proceeds to a contested hearing as currently. Any papers regarding settlement proposals are returned at the end of the FDR.

Fourteen days before any final hearing the applicant must file and serve a statement setting out concise details, including the amount involved and the orders sought. The respondent must within 7 days of receipt of the applicant's statement, file and serve a statement setting out the orders he seeks.

New costs provisions post June 2000

The new rules introduce two new specific provisions regarding the effect of negotiations and costs. They re-impose the obligation to negotiate as dealt with above (page 113) but the new rules add a new twist. They provide the following.

- Either party may make an offer on a 'without prejudice except as to costs' basis.

- ■ If the order made is more advantageous than the offer made, then the court must, unless it is unjust, order the other party to pay the costs from a date 28 days after the offer is made.
- ■ Where both parties have made offers and the court order is more advantageous than both the offers made, the court can:
  - − order interest on all or part of the lump sum (interest to be not more than 10% above base rate);
  - − order indemnity costs and interest on the costs.

New interim hearings

After June 2000 when a party wants an interim order, he may make an application for maintenance pending suit or an interim order on 14 days notice. If the application is made before the Form E is filed, the applicant must serve a draft order and a short sworn statement explaining why the order is required and including details of his means. The respondent must file a sworn statement about his means 7 days before the hearing.

New pension law

Pension splitting already exists whereby one party is awarded part of the pension of the other, although the fund remains in the original person's name. The next stage is pension sharing, currently expected in 2000 or possibly 2001. This will give the court the power to divide the pension fund between the parties at the time of the financial settlement.

Where the pensions are a significant matrimonial asset and retirement is likely within the next few years, the new rules will assist the party claiming the pension.

The new rules will apply to cases where the divorce petition and financial application are issued after the date of implementation.

Pre-nuptial agreements

A pre-nuptial agreement is one entered into before marriage and in contemplation of marriage to set out the agreement between the parties as to how they are to deal with their financial affairs, particularly in the event that the parties later separate and divorce.

In parts of Europe, pre-nuptial agreements are legally binding and the parties can agree how the court should deal with the capital assets on a divorce. One common method is to agree that property brought into the marriage by each party or inherited during the marriage should remain the property of that person and that only the property generated during the marriage should be available to be divided on divorce.

People already make pre-nuptial agreements in England and Wales and the court treats the agreement as being one of the relevant factors when considering the financial settlement. It is not, however, bound to follow the agreement.

The government is considering making pre-nuptial agreements legal, rather than of evidential interest. There will be safeguards which are likely to include a review whenever either party becomes incapacitated, when a child is born and in any event after five years, and if there is no review at the appropriate time, an automatic lapse of the agreement.

Child support

In July 1999, a White Paper proposed fundamental changes to the Child Support Act. The changes will stop the present complex mathematical calculation and replace them with a clear and easy method of calculation of child support. The changes are that a parent with whom the child or children do not live will pay 15% of his net income if he has one child, 20% for two children and 25% for three or more children. Allowances will be made for families on low incomes and where there are step children or second families. The changes are expected to apply to new cases after the Act comes into force in about 2001. At present it is not intended to have any ceiling on the upper level of maintenance. There will be a reduction to the child support figure if the children spend over 104 days per annum with the absent parent. It is intended to extend the power to enforce the assessments and there will be new criminal powers if a person refuses to co-operate.

The Human Rights Act 1998

This Act introduces the concepts of the European Convention on Human Rights into English law. While not directly applicable to domestic divorce law, the Act is likely to have an increasing influence in the way in which the English law approaches divorce law, and in particular the individual rights of the family within the marriage. The effect of European law has already had an effect on the way the English court approaches difficulties over children and child abduction.

Conclusion

Going through the divorce process is never easy, but remember, that two years after the divorce when you look back, it will have been worthwhile. There is life after divorce.

APPENDIX

Useful addresses

Finding a Solicitor

- Law Society of England and Wales, 113 Chancery Lane, London WC2A 1PL. Telephone 020 7242 1222 maintains a register of accredited Family Lawyers and lists of lawyers by location.
- The Solicitors' Family Law Association maintains lists of local members who subscribe to its code of practice and has its own accreditation scheme and can provide a list of accredited lawyers. Contact: P.O. Box 302 Orpington, Kent BR6 8QX. Telephone 01689 850227.
- Citizens Advice Bureau maintain lists of local solicitors who will undertake divorce and legal aid work.

Finding a counsellor

- Relate, see local Yellow Pages.
- London Marriage Guidance, 76a New Cavendish Street, London W1M 7LB. Telephone 020 7580 1087.
- Tavistock Marital Studies Institute, 120 Belsize Lane London NW3 5BA. Telephone 020 7447 3725.
- Couple Counselling Service, run by the Society of Psychology Marital Therapy. Telephone 0870 9024878.
- Jewish Counselling Service, 25 Ravenshurst Avenue, London NW4 4EE. Telephone 020 8203 6311.
- Yellow pages – under Counselling & Advice.
- Through local recommendation such as GP.

Finding a mediator

■ UK College of Family Mediators, Stephenson Way London, NW1 2HD. Telephone 020 7391 9162.

■ Family Mediator's Association, 1 Wyvil Court, London SW1 0EB. Telephone 020 7881 9400.

■ Solicitor's Family Law Association mediation panel as above.

Courts

■ Principal Registry of the Family Division, First Avenue House, 42–49, High Holborn, London WC1V 6NP. Telephone 020 7936 1500.

■ High Court of Justice, Family Division, Royal Courts of Justice, Strand, London WC2A 2LL. Telephone 020 7947 6000. (Or District Registry if outside London – see telephone directory.

■ Local county courts – see Local telephone directory.

Organisations that may help

■ Families need Fathers, 134–146 Curtain Road, London EC2A 3AR. Telephone 020 7613 5060.

■ National Stepfamily Association Chapel House, 18 Hatton Place, London EC1N 8AU. Telephone 020 7209 2460.

■ Family Law Bar Association, Queen Elizabeth Building, Temple, London EC4Y 9BS.

Court forms

■ Desktop Lawyer produce court forms on the web at a charge – **www.desktoplawyer.freeserve.net/law**

■ Oyez, Oyez House, 7 Spa Road, London SE16. Telephone 020 8343 6270.

Some terms defined

Calderbank: a without prejudice letter which the court can see when deciding costs.

Clean break: where all the on-going financial claims against the other cease.

Decree absolute: the final order of divorce.

Decree nisi: the first stage of divorce.

Duxbury: the calculation of the capitalisation of maintenance.

Financial relief: the application for the financial settlement including income and capital.

Form E: the sworn financial statement required under the pilot scheme and from June 2000, the nationwide Pilot Scheme.

Form M1: statement of financial information required to obtain a consent order.

Petition: the document filed with the court setting out the history of the marriage and setting out the basis on which a divorce is sought.

Petitioner: the person who files the divorce.

Respondent: the party against whom the divorce is sought.

Court fees

- On filing the divorce petition £150.
- On applying for the decree nisi nil.
- On filing the decree absolute £30.
- On filing the application for financial relief (Form A) £80.
- On filing the agreed order for financial relief/ or dismissal £30.
- Children's application £80.
- Wardship £120.

INDEX